Bathroom Planning and Remodeling

Joseph F. Schram

Ideals Publishing Corp.
Milwaukee, Wisconsin

Table of Contents

ISBN 0-8249-6102-1

Copyright © 1981 by Ideals Publishing Corporation

All rights reserved. This book or parts thereof, may not be reproduced in any form without permission of the copyright owners. Printed and bound in the United States of America. Published simultaneously in Canada.

Published by Ideals Publishing Corporation
11315 Watertown Plank Road
Milwaukee, Wisconsin 53226

Editor, David Schansberg

Cover photo courtesy of Kohler

SUCCESSFUL
HOME IMPROVEMENT SERIES

Bathroom Planning and Remodeling
Kitchen Planning and Remodeling
Space Saving Shelves and Built-ins
Finishing Off Additional Rooms
Finding and Fixing the Older Home
Money Saving Home Repair Guide
Homeowner's Guide to Tools
Homeowner's Guide to Electrical Wiring
Homeowner's Guide to Plumbing
Homeowner's Guide to Roofing and Siding
Homeowner's Guide to Fireplaces
Home Plans for the '80s
How to Build Your Own Home

Planning and Remodeling Your Bathroom

Planning a new bathroom or remodeling an existing one begins with designing a floor plan that will suit your family's needs and desires. Often this decision will be made for you for the most part by the amount of space available; but if you are beginning from "scratch," you will find a wide latitude in what you can plan and the products available.

In planning a bathroom for a new home or in adding a complete new bathroom to an existing dwelling, it is good to begin by asking yourself a number of questions. The answers will provide you, and those assisting you in the project, with necessary facts and objectives to be incorporated into the overall plan. The most important questions to be considered are:

- What area of the home will be served by this bathroom?
- Who will be the principal users of the bathroom—Parents? Children? Guests?
- Will this bathroom be an integral part of the master suite, or should it be "family" in nature and serve several bedrooms adjacent to its location?
- How much space can be allotted to the new bathroom?
- What is the maximum cost figure that can be considered?
- What basic fixtures are necessary in the new room? Tub or shower?
- How much space should be planned for bathroom storage?
- Will the room be used for other than normal bathroom purposes—will it also serve as an exercise room, an added place to relax, or an extension of the master suite?

In this section of *Bathroom Planning and Remodeling* you will find photographs and floor plans of popular contemporary bathroom designs. These plans have been carefully designed with regard to fixture placement, necessary storage, movement within the room, possible use by more than one person at a time, location of doors and windows, and several other factors.

While the most economical plumbing arrangement incorporates all fixtures on a single wall, this greatly reduces the design and use acceptability of the room and is often thereby discarded in favor of using one or more additional "wet" walls.

The floor plans in this section can be used in designing your new or remodeled bath. Keep in mind that the ideas presented can be combined and expanded to suit your particular needs or tastes.

The Master Suite Bath

Builders, architects, and decorators have found the master bedroom-bathroom suite to be a key factor in attracting new home sales. This is especially true when the price of the home is $100,000 or more and the buyer has already owned a "tract" home with a cramped minimum three-fixture bathroom.

Today's master suite may be viewed as a private living area for the "master" and "mistress" of the home, geared to individual or combined interests. Personal preference and need is the key to the design of this type of bedroom-bathroom area. Attention, however, should be given to including:

- Single or double lavatory bowls in easy-to-maintain countertops with cabinets which provide ample storage area for common bathroom items such as towels, cosmetics, tissue, etc.
- Ample storage area for his and her clothes, shoes and accessories. You'll note the dressing room approach in many of the accompanying floor plans. The tub or shower and toilet have been "compartmentalized" away from the dressing area, which includes the wash basin and vanity.
- Separate or combination bathtub-shower units to maintain the flexibility of the bathroom, both now and in the event of a future sale of the dwelling. All showers and no bathtub will be a drawback when reselling the home.

The Compartmented Bathroom

Compartmented bathrooms which can serve two or more persons at the same time increase the room's efficiency and often require little more floor space than an open floor plan. New and remodeled bathrooms can be divided into compartments by installing hinged or sliding doors, screens, or partitions. The basic compartmented bath separates the lavatory from the tub and water closet to allow two people simultaneous use of the room. More elaborate bathrooms offer twin-basin lavatories, one or two separate water closets, and a tub or shower in still another section of the room.

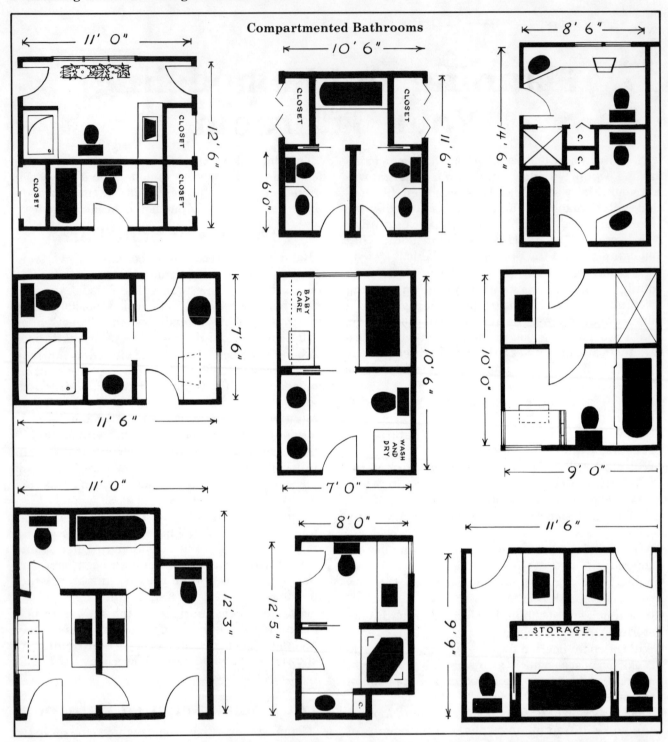

Compartmented Bathrooms

The Garden Bathroom

Your choice of compartmented bathrooms will depend upon the number of persons who may need to use it at the same time, and the floor space available. Care should be taken that swinging doors do not inconvenience those using the room.

The Garden Bathroom

The impact of California home design on building styles in recent years has resulted in national accept-

ance of and desire for the garden bathroom—affording the user a garden view, a private patio, or a combination of both.

The glass wall or sliding glass door which opens onto a private garden or patio gives the room a larger, more luxurious aspect. Tempered glass is recommended, and in many areas required, by local building codes. Glass areas needn't be confined to walls free of plumbing fixtures. Delightful settings can be obtained by placing viewing windows above

Garden Bathrooms

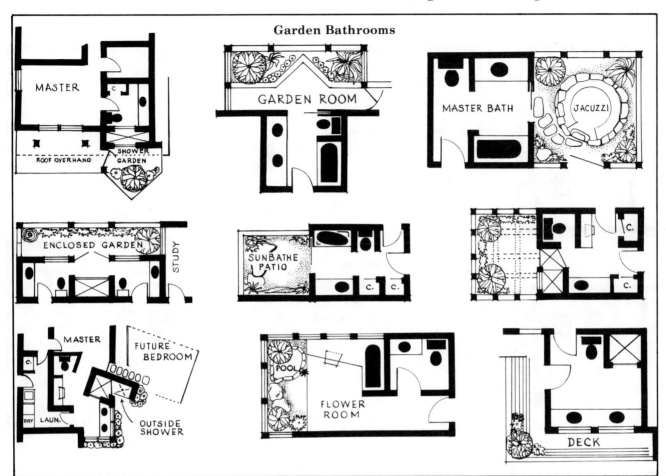

built-in vanities and adjacent to sunken or raised tubs or tub-shower combinations. If the bath garden is entirely secluded, the scene can be enhanced with outdoor lighting, thus keeping the large expanse of glass from appearing black and cold at night. Draw draperies can be installed in the bathroom for night privacy, if the drapes are not close to the shower.

Screens, fences, and plantings furnish the privacy necessary to a garden bathroom. The garden itself may be large enough for sunbathing and relaxation, or it may be so small as to offer a view of only a few selected plant groupings from the bathroom proper.

Some garden bathrooms offer the option of indoor or outdoor showering by including a second shower on the outside bath wall. This can be especially convenient when the garden is near a swimming pool, so that swimmers can shower without entering the bathroom.

Plantings in the patio, bathroom, or garden should be selected for their decorative appeal and their ability to grow in confined space. Most house plants thrive in the warm, humid atmosphere of a bathroom. Some of the most successful are: orchids, Chinese evergreen, African violets, philodendron, grape ivy, and fittonia. Flowers and shrubs to be used in

outside gardens should be chosen with climate in mind in order to avoid bare gray branches in the winter or parched, wilted leaves in the summer. Position plants so they receive ample sunlight (or a proper artificial substitute), and so that shower water does not strike them, bruising the foliage or causing rot.

The Powder Room or Lavatory

Half-baths, better known as the powder room or lavatory, have become extremely handy in homes of all sizes. These rooms can be located in areas convenient to the living area of a home, i.e., the kitchen, den, and family room. The powder room has no bathtub while providing the other major bathroom fixtures, namely the water closet and lavatory basin. If the primary users are to be children, this room can be designed for minimum maintenance. It can be more formally decorated if it will serve adults and guests.

Because you won't have to contend with the water vapor problem created by a tub or shower, you can use decorative objects in a powder room that would not be practical in a family bath. Chain lamps, picture-frame mirrors, and cabinets enhance the setting and can give an impression of spaciousness. Skylights are often used in powder rooms to provide

Lavatories

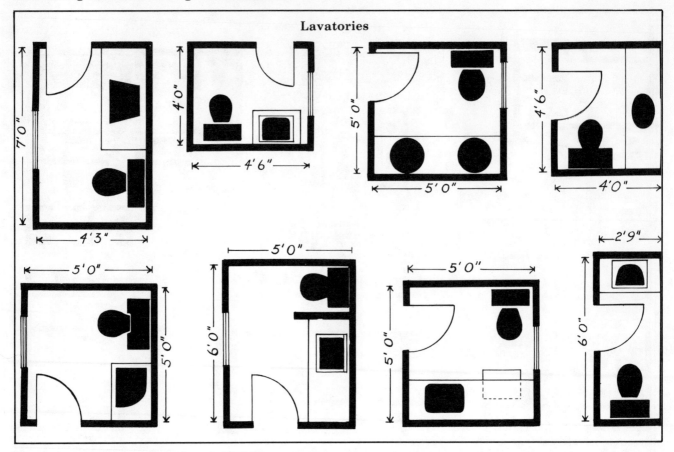

natural illumination, especially in rooms without windows. Combination light fixture-exhaust fans are also popular.

Care should be taken that the door swings toward a clear wall space whenever possible and not against the water closet or lavatory.

Children's Bath

The children's bath should be a room that is easily cleaned. Surfaces should withstand splashing, spotting, and dripping; tile is therefore more practical than carpeting.

The children's bath should be readily accessible from children's bedrooms. Door locks should be the type that can be opened from outside the bathroom if necessary.

Manufacturers recommend using standard-size fixtures for the children's bathroom, along with built-in steps or stools to bring the wash basin within reach of a child's shorter arms. Wash basins can be installed at a lower height, but as the children grow the installation would be impractical and would have to be replaced. Single-handle faucets are simpler and safer than separate hot and cold water controls which require mixing the water to the desired temperature. Showers can include two shower heads. The top one can be plugged initially

with the lower one operative for youngsters. As the children grow, the lower one can be plugged and the upper one put into use. Electrical plans for this type of bathroom should include a built-in night light. All forms of ceiling fans and heaters should be operated by a timer control to shut the units off if the children forget.

If the water closet stall is equipped with a door, the door should swing outward and be a minimum of 32 inches wide. Minimum depth of the stall should be 60 inches, and the total width should be at least 36 inches to allow for heavy-duty 4-foot-long grab-safety bars on each side of the toilet. The walls can enclose the area from floor to ceiling, or partial-height walls can flank the water closet.

Floor- or wall-mounted toilet bowls should be 18 inches in height from rim to floor, and the front edge should be no more than 29¾ inches from the wall. Grab bars are centered on the front edge of the bowl to give two feet of bar area in front of and two feet alongside of the bowl.

Bathtubs with built-in grip rails are recommended. The tub models available can be recessed between three walls or, for models which have no apron, may be installed as a peninsula in the room. Slip-free bottoms are a must, preferably a ridged surface rather than a mat which could slide when wet.

Master Bathrooms

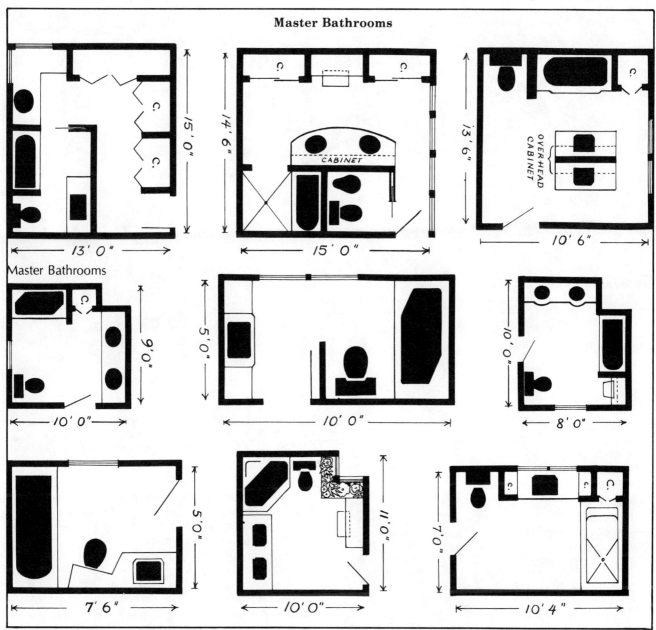

15' 0"

14' 6"

13' 6"

CABINET

13' 0"

15' 0"

OVER-HEAD CABINET

10' 6"

Master Bathrooms

9' 0"

5' 0"

10' 0"

10' 0"

10' 0"

8' 0"

5' 0"

11' 0"

7' 0"

7' 6"

10' 0"

10' 4"

White stucco walls, shutters, and rich dark beams were used to create this Mediterranean bathroom. The fixtures are green, as is the tile floor. Photo courtesy of American-Standard

Planned for children's needs from infancy through the teens, this bathroom has a wide countertop alongside the deep lavatory. The bottom drawer pulls out to become a step and can be easily converted to conventional drawer space at a later time. A recessed shelf above the towels accommodates plastic glasses. A folding door and companion lavatory on one side of the wall, and second lavatory with bath on other side prevent tie-ups as children mature.

A sliding pocket door converts this master bath into two separate, private areas. Louvered doors, stained to match the paneling on the walls, conceal his and her medicine cabinets on each side of the mirror. The soffit houses fluorescent fixtures illuminating the vanity area. Standard window shutters, mounted on a shower track with louvers slanted inward, add to the rugged appearance established by the paneling. Photo courtesy of Marlite

It's just a matter of steps between this master bathroom and bedroom. To emphasize the modern decor, a large vanity was included on the main wall, which also features a gold-crafted mural panel. Plastic-finished paneling surfaces the remainder of the wall area, and the ceiling is a wall-to-wall, luminous grid system. Photo courtesy of Marlite

The compartmented water closet area of this garden bathroom can be closed off via folding panel doors sur-faced in the same vinyl material as surrounding walls. Photo courtesy of American-Standard

Use of the corner area for lavatory installation leaves room for a sit-down area in this powder room, as well as storage space below the basin. Plastic-finished planks were used for the walls, and gold and black marble-patterned plastic laminate for the countertop. Photo courtesy of Marlite

"Her" area of the master bathroom suite in this home features a vanity counter with special features—a jewelry drawer, concealed storage, glass shelves, and a mirrored make-up compartment illuminated from below. Photo courtesy of Eljer

A compartmented water closet area and twin self-rimming lavatories enable two people to use this bathroom simultaneously. A full-length mirror is mounted on the clothes closet at left. The window treatment above the water closet is repeated in the tub area. Photo courtesy of Kohler

This compartmented bathroom features an elevated bathtub that can be separated from the dressing area and water closet by draperies. Photo courtesy of Tile Council of America

This beautiful bathroom (upper left) was finished off at one end of an unfinished attic. The bathtub is recessed in the wall and is flanked by a large skylight. Photo courtesy of Quaker Maid

Another good example of an attic bathroom (lower left) features an oversized oval bathtub with carpeted surround. The stained-glass dormer window adds to the privacy of this attractive master bedroom. Photo courtesy of Quaker Maid

Evocative of the Orient, this bath has sliding glass shoji screens enclosing the shower stall and serving as a passageway from the vanity to the tub area, which is decorated as an indoor Japanese garden. The sunken tub is lined with 2 x 2 unglazed ceramic mosaics. The vanity with two under-the-counter basins and center dressing table is topped with plastic laminate. Japanese architecture is presently a strong influence on bathroom design in the United States. Photo courtesy of American Olean Tile

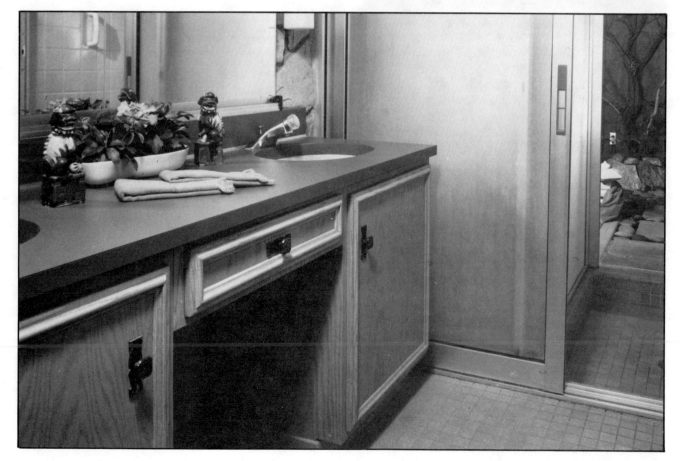

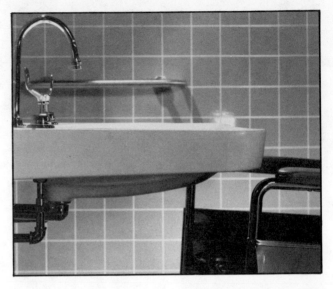

Art objects need not be confined to the living and dining rooms. Both built-in and free-standing display units add to this small bathroom setting. Photo courtesy of American-Standard

Especially designed for wheelchair patients, this lavatory has a roll-under design which eliminates possible interference of the legs or chair with water supplies, pipe, or lavatory. The fixture is available, with punching, on 12-inch centers for wrist handles or 4-inch centers for push-pull fittings. Photo courtesy of American-Standard

Fixed tempered glass along the back and one end of the bathtub afford the bather a private garden view. The tub is six feet long and three feet wide with gently sloping back for reclining ease. Photo courtesy of Kohler

Features for the Elderly or the Handicapped

Bathrooms designed for retirement homes should stress safety, convenience, and easy maintenance. Walls, floors, and accessories should eliminate the need for periodic refinishing or complicated maintenance. Plastic laminates, ceramic tile, and plastic-coated hardboard are the most popular and effective materials for this type of bathroom.

In designing a new retirement bathroom, make the doorway wide enough to accommodate a wheelchair and select a lock style that will allow the door to be opened from the outside in an emergency. Door knobs and light swiches should be 36 inches above floor level. Knobs and switches at a lower level require stooping, which might strain already painful muscles. Floors should be of a nonslip material, and if carpeting is used it should be taped to the floor. Scatter rugs are dangerous and should be avoided. Bathtubs and shower stalls should include a built-in seat or ledge. Both installations should include sturdy grab bars at both sitting and standing height. Grab bars are also desirable on either side of the toilet. Extra-large medicine cabinets are recommended, so that all medicines are clearly visible.

Brighter illumination than usual from both natural and artificial sources adds safety and convenience. Single-handle lavatory and shower controls are easiest to operate. The installation of a pressure and temperature control valve in the shower prevents accidental blasts of hot or cold water.

Planning and adding special bathroom features for a physically handicapped person requires the selection of special plumbing fixtures suited to the user's needs. The fixtures should provide maximum convenience for the patient.

Lavatory installations with special fixtures for easy access to a wheelchair patient are available. Some models have curved front rims for additional

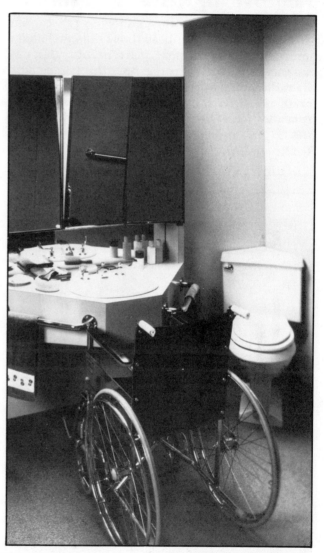

Planned to provide easy access for wheelchairs or crutches, this bathroom designed for the handicapped person includes an 18-inch-high corner toilet. The lavatory drop-in bowl is fitted with wrist-action handles for easier use by an arthritic individual. The center mirror is adjustable for use when sitting down or standing up. Heavy-duty grab bars double as towel bars. Photo courtesy of Eljer

Toilets for use by senior citizens and handicapped persons should have extra height from the floor to the top of the rim. The siphon jet unit has an elongated bowl, large water area, and large passageway. The fixture comes in white and in a variety of colors. Photo courtesy of Kohler

comfort and convenience. The rim-to-floor measurement should be 34 inches and fittings should be equipped with 4-inch wrist controls. Standard lavatory size for this type of installation is a 20-inch width and a 27-inch depth. A concealed arm support is required for the fixture.

Shower stalls for the physically handicapped should be 36 inches wide and 36 inches deep, and be equipped with an L-shaped, heavy-duty grab bar. All fittings should be readily accessible. A folding seat, if used, must be raised or lowered without difficulty.

Seven Inexpensive Ways to Improve an Existing Bathroom

The seven basic bathrooms shown on these pages are typical of the countless thousands included in homes built over the past quarter-century. In each instance, a minor rearrangement as suggested by Eljer Plumbingware results in more usable space for the modern family. The improvements range from addition of vanity cabinets and medicine cabinets to relocation of fixtures for a more efficient floor plan. Always be on the lookout for places where you can add cabinets and storage.

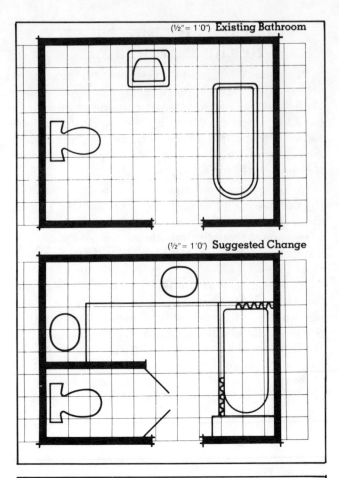

(½" = 1'0") **Existing Bathroom**

(½" = 1'0") **Suggested Change**

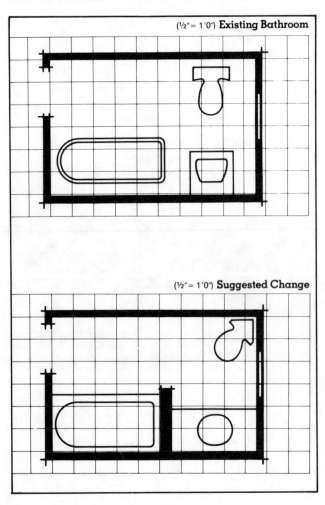

(½" = 1'0") **Existing Bathroom**

(½" = 1'0") **Suggested Change**

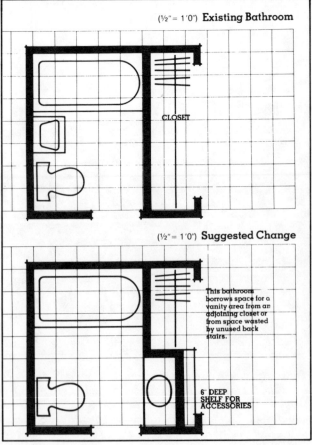

(½" = 1'0") **Existing Bathroom**

CLOSET

(½" = 1'0") **Suggested Change**

This bathroom borrows space for a vanity area from an adjoining closet or from space wasted by unused back stairs.

6" DEEP SHELF FOR ACCESSORIES

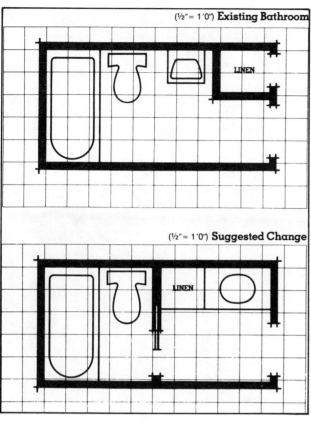

(½" = 1'0") **Existing Bathroom**

LINEN

(½" = 1'0") **Suggested Change**

LINEN

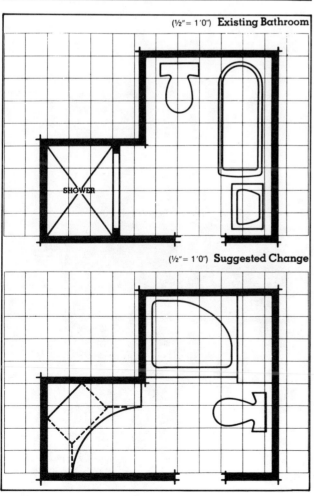

(½" = 1'0") **Existing Bathroom**

SHOWER

(½" = 1'0") **Suggested Change**

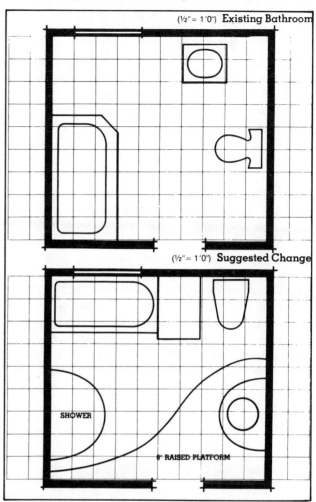

(½" = 1'0") **Existing Bathroom**

(½" = 1'0") **Suggested Change**

SHOWER

6" RAISED PLATFORM

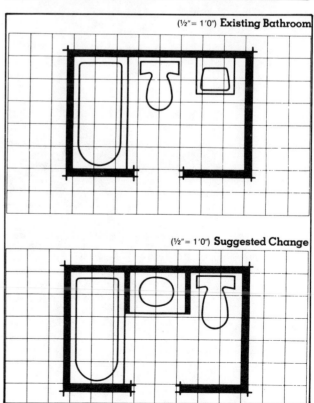

(½" = 1'0") **Existing Bathroom**

(½" = 1'0") **Suggested Change**

What Remodeling Can Accomplish

Bathroom remodeling can accomplish miracles as depicted here in the renewal of an 1880-vintage master bathroom in Philadelphia. The original fixtures were installed during World War I. The newest fixture was the pedestal lavatory.

A previous remodeling replaced the old hot-water radiator with a more modern under-the-window unit. The old corner medicine cabinet had been removed, but paint continued to peel, and the floor tiles heaved as the tileboard bulged.

Using a modern layout in the same space, a tub was sunk into an unused back stairwell and was supported by steel I-beams resting on iron braces bolted to the joists. Beyond the arch, the toilet was placed to one side, with a new linen closet occupying the other side. Window size was reduced.

On the right side of the bathroom a long decorative, plastic laminate countertop houses twin self-rimming lavatories above added storage area. Vinyl wall covering and American Olean ceramic tile were used for the walls, with large 12-inch-square tiles for the floor.

Color in the Bathroom

Color and accessories are the decorator's prime allies in achieving a beautiful bathroom. Every item in the bathroom contributes to the total design and thus must be given attention and consideration in relation to the effect desired.

Most manufacturers of bathroom fixtures offer both pastel and bright accent colors in addition to standard white units. Similarly named colors vary in shading or intensity from firm to firm. If possible you should select complete sets of fixtures from a single manufacturer in order to insure consistent color match. Bright and bold colors have taken over the bathroom in recent years, just as they have the kitchen and other rooms of the modern home. Rather than relying on the towels to provide the color, designers use the major elements, the fixtures, to set the scene, and then design and build around them for the finished setting.

The colors chosen for the fixtures determine to a large extent the decorative scheme for the floor, walls, ceiling, and accessories. Suppliers and designers recommend that you choose a wall color that harmonizes with the fixtures, rather than trying to match it exactly. Light colors tend to make bathrooms appear larger and brighter. They also increase room illumination, making it easier to shave and apply makeup.

Because surfaces such as floors, countertops, and walls (if they are surfaced with plastic laminate or ceramic tile) must be considered at least semi-permanent and probably will not be changed very often, they should complement the fixtures. Painted walls and those finished with flexible materials can be redecorated more easily, allowing a wider range of selection.

Carpeting has become acceptable and desirable in the bathroom. Select a carpet that has a waterproof membrane between the fiber and the backing material. This will prevent water damage to the carpeting and flooring beneath it. Generally, carpeting should be the same color as that in the bedroom if the bathroom is part of a master suite or a combination dressing room-bath arrangement. Likewise, a bathroom opening off a hall should be compatible with the hall wall, floor, and ceiling colors.

The color most often chosen for ceilings is white, because it reflects more light and plays a neutral role in the total color scheme. If wood or wood paneling is used for the ceiling, or if the ceiling is painted a dark color, plan to provide more lighting to counteract the lower reflection given by the darker ceiling.

Manufacturers, shelter magazines, and the color section in this book offer a wealth of color schemes for the bathroom. Each incorporates the brand-name fixture color to keep you from going astray. Should you decide to select a new color scheme, first obtain a Color Wheel from a local art store. It puts colors in relationship to each other so that you can see for yourself which colors you like. Here are a few color tips:

- Complementary colors: You can decorate with complementary colors that are opposites on the color wheel, red and green; blue and orange; yellow and violet. If you choose a complementary color scheme, don't use both colors at full strength, or intensity. For instance, with a vivid red, use a dark, grayed green. For a strong purple, bring in a pale gold, not butter yellow. In using complementary colors, contrast results in design impact.
- Analogous colors: You can use colors that are next to each other on the color wheel, analogous or adjacent colors: orange, yellow-orange, and yellow; green, yellow-green, and yellow; violet, red-violet, and blue-violet. These color schemes are vibrant, and usually great fun to work out. Contrast is minimal.
- Monochromatic colors: You may decide to use only one color in varying shades and intensities. These hues are called monochromatic colors, and can be one of the easiest and often most effective types of color plans. Everything is tied together by the bond of color. For instance, a blue bathroom could include pale sky blue, delphinium blue, and a touch of navy blue for accent. Monochromatic schemes resemble music—many variations on a theme.
- Nature's colors: Keep in mind that there are no discordant colors in nature. Blue and green are always together. A color scheme can be built from a flower, a bowl of fresh fruit, a basket of vegetables, the shades of a mottled rock formation. Your catalyst for a color scheme might be a fabric or a print: a gay chintz or a provincial print could key everything else in the room.

Use of a single-pattern, decorative plastic laminate for the walls, tub recess, soffit, vanity, and countertop resulted in this bathroom design by Edmund Moytka, A.I.D. Photo courtesy of Formica

Walls, Ceilings, Floors, and Plumbing Systems

Walls and Ceilings

Wall surfaces in the bathroom should be moisture resistant and easy to maintain. Because most bathrooms are fairly small, it is best to use the same wall covering throughout. This is not a hard and fast rule, however.

In choosing bathroom wall surfacing, it is a good idea to select a material, color, or pattern compatible with the decorating scheme used in adjoining rooms. This can be accomplished with color, textures, and choice of materials. Wall surfaces commonly found in bathrooms include decorative plastic laminates, ceramic tile, plastic tile, enamel-painted plaster, or gypsum wallboard, and vinyl wall coverings. Wallpaper and fabric can be purchased with a washable and waterproof surface, or waterproof treatment can be applied following installation. Generally, wallpaper is only practical in lavatories and powder rooms where moisture is not produced by tub or shower bathing.

Most bathroom walls are finished in pastel or light colors. If you decide to use a dark color or a simulated dark wood finish, keep in mind that this will absorb more natural and artificial light. You may need additional lighting to compensate for the dark walls. The most critical wall area in the bathroom is that around a tub or shower stall. When tile is to be applied, vinyl-surfaced gypsum wallboard, waterproof plaster, or marine plywood is first applied to the framing. Vinyl wallboard comes in one piece that can be scored to fit around three sides of the tub, but in shower stalls this material must be carefully taped at all seams.

Both plastic and ceramic should be applied with water-resistant adhesives. Plastic laminates and predecorated tempered hardboard are also used for tub and shower area walls, and again, special care should be given to obtaining leakproof joints.

Decorative Plastic Laminates Decorative high-pressure laminated plastic has become one of the most frequently used materials in today's bathroom. This durable product is suitable for countertop surfaces, walls, bathtub surrounds, and as a vertical surfacing for many decorator-styled vanities and cabinets.

Laminated plastic was developed in the early 1900s as an electrical insulating material. Decorative plastic laminate was born when the top layer of paper in the laminate "sandwich" was printed with a design before being bonded into the plastic. The design, visible through the transparent plastic-resin surface, provides the material's beauty. Today's decorative plastic laminate is available in literally hundreds of solid colors, wood grains, patterns, and a variety of textured and three-dimensional surfaces. It provides virtually unlimited design possibilities.

Laminated plastic surfaces are almost abuse-proof in normal use. They are easily cared for with a damp cloth and retain their beauty year after year with no refinishing required. The material is also available in a "cigarette proof" grade. Impacts that dent wood, and cuts, scratches, and abrasions that mar paints and lacquers, hardly affect laminated plastic. The material is manufactured in large sheets that can be cut to fit most any shape. Large areas may be covered with seamless or almost seamless surfaces, and by using "postforming" techniques common to cabinet makers, laminated plastics may also be applied to many curved surfaces.

Ceramic Tile Ceramic tile's popularity as a covering for bathroom floors and walls is due to its beauty, ease of maintenance, and resistance to water. Ceramic tile is produced by mixing clays that are baked at extremely high temperatures, and comes in several forms:

• Glazed tile is composed of metallic oxides and ceramic stains which give the tile surface color and texture. This kind of tile can be found in sizes ranging from 1 inch square to 12 inches square, and in a vast variety of shapes. Colors range over the entire palette, with the very bright colors less resistant to wear. Gloss, matte, and crystalline glazes are suitable for interior walls and vanity tops. Crystalline and certain other glazes may also be used on floors. Thicknesses are available from $3/8$ to $5/16$ of an inch. Installation costs will range from $1.30 to $4.00 per square foot for $4\frac{1}{4}$-inch tile, depending upon the method of installa-

Redi-Set pregrouted ceramic tile sheets, approximately two square feet, are easily put into place over gypsum wallboard. The grout joints are filled at the factory with a flexible silicone-rubber grout which will not mildew, stain, or crack with building movement. After all sheets are in place, the same grout material is used to finish the installation. Photo courtesy of American Olean

tion and size of the job. The more elaborate shapes and designs may cost as high as $10 per square foot to install.

• Ceramic mosaics are usually small, unglazed solid chunks with color in the body of the tile. They come in sizes 1 x 1, 1 x 2, and 2 x 2 inches. A broad color choice exists, affording great design flexibility with these unit sizes, which may be combined in many patterns and colors. The only limitation on design is imagination. The average thickness is ¼ inch. The ceramics are usually mounted into sheets measuring 1 x 2 feet, either on paper or back-mounted. Ceramic mosaics are suitable for interior and exterior floors and walls. Porcelain tile will absorb less than ½ percent moisture, is frost-proof, and highly wear-resistant. The natural clay tile has a rich, natural appearance but is more porous and more likely to stain. These tiles need never be waxed, but a sealer is sometimes used to protect the cement joints. Cost of installation will vary from $1.50 to $3.15 per square foot, depending upon cost of tile (varying with color, size, and design) and method of installation, with an average of $1.75 to $2.00 per square foot.

• Quarry tile is available in warm, earthy shades, generally ranging from beige to dark, rich brown.

Material combinations in today's bathrooms often include natural wood, ceramic tile, decorative plastic laminates, flexible vinyl, plastics, and carpeting. Each plays an important role in minimizing upkeep as well as adding to the overall decor. Photo courtesy of American-Standard

The tiles are usually unglazed, and the color is integral throughout the tile body. Some manufacturers incorporate a color stain. Sizes range from 4 x 4 inches to 8 x 8 inches and a number of shapes are available, including hexagon, octagon, and provincial. Quarry tile is usually ½ inch thick and is made by the extrusion process from natural clay or shale. Quarry tile is suitable for residential floors and is highly resistant to wear from abrasion. Originally used primarily in commercial installations, quarry tile is now used extensively in homes because its warm, natural tone lends itself to either the contemporary or provincial look. Cost of installation will range from $1.65 to $3.25 per square foot. Curved, special shapes are more time-consuming to install and will cost slightly more.

Ceramic tile was used in this small bathroom for walls, tub periphery, and vanity countertops. Photo courtesy of   *Tile Council of America*

Installation of Ceramic Tile

Ceramic tile increases in popularity each year as more and more people discover its beauty, durability, and easy maintenance. Tile can be used for floors, walls, countertops, tub surrounds and even ceilings. Installation is relatively easy but a bit dirty. The installation sequence for tile sheets on the following pages is courtesy of American Olean Tile.

1—Abrade laminated top with coarse sandpaper wrapped around a block.

2—Plan layout of tile sheets allowing for cove base and trim. Plan as few cuts as possible.

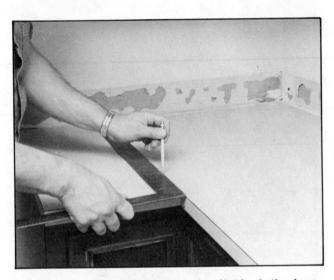

3—Draw lines for installation of individual tile sheets.

4—Spread epoxy adhesive with notched trowel over entire surface.

5—Start installation of tile in a corner beginning with trim.

6—Begin installing sheets making sure to align all joints carefully.

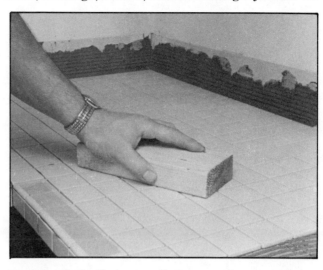

7—Seat tile firmly in epoxy adhesive by tapping with a wooden block.

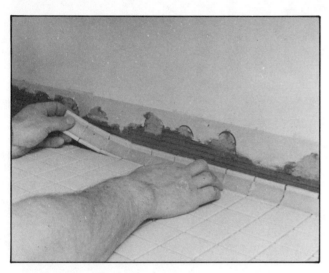

8—Apply cove base trim at back of counter.

9—Tile can be cut with a mechanical cutter. They may be rented from some building supply stores.

10—Nip tile to shape as needed.

11—Install corner cove trim.

12—Wait 24 hours after setting tile, then grout using a rubber faced trowel.

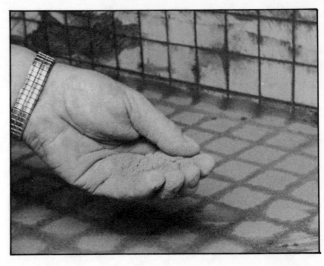

13—Sprinkle dry grout over entire surface to absorb all excess moisture.

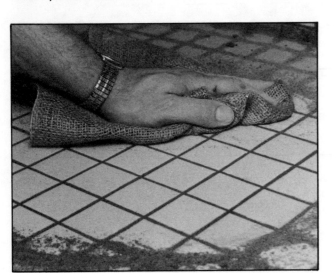

14—Rub surface with dry burlap to compact joints.

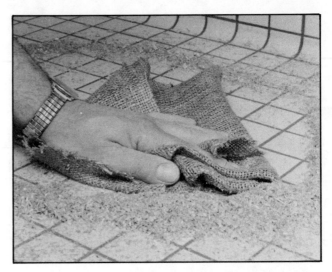

15—Dampen sawdust with mild acid/water solution and rub grouted tile with burlap to clean tile surface.

The greater freedom in decorating home interiors has invaded the bathroom with thousands of home-owners favoring colorful wallcoverings over the customary plain paint surfaces.

Wallcoverings do wonders in transforming old bathrooms to attractive new rooms. Hung like wallpaper, the newer vinyl-coated and vinyl-backed materials provide geometrics, textures, stripes, ethnic looks, florals, and natural stylings in hundreds of colors.

The combinations of plastic coating and fabric backing have greatly increased the popularity of bathroom wallcoverings. Aside from being resistant to bathroom moisture, these materials are both easy to install (over gypsum wallboard, plaster, and masonry) and may be washed with a sponge.

Vinyl wall coverings may be machine printed or hand printed, with the machine-printed type having the advantage of easier removal from the wall when redecorating is desired. With the machine type, the vinyl layer separates from its backing when pulled off, leaving the base for the next covering. With cloth-backed vinyls, various cloths such as canvas and gauze are used for vinyl backing and vinyl comes in gauges ranging from thick to thin, some almost board-like. A wide variety of textured effects are worked into cloth-backed vinyls, many of them effective simulations of silk, moire, velvet, and wood.

Perhaps the newest in bathroom wallcoverings is the foil-less, foil created with Mylar to provide a subtle gleam not found in the shinier foils of the

Decorative rough-hewn wood beams and wood parquet flooring are augmented by wood shutters and the vanity in this master bathroom. Washable pull drapes are used *for the fiberglass shower recess as well as the water closet compartment. Photo courtesy of Universal-Rundle*

past. The metallic finish is overlaid with textures and patterns so that only a portion of the shiny material shows through, resulting in a softer, more subdued reflection which gleams rather than glares.

Unlike foils of the past, the new collection is scrubbable as well as strippable. Also unlike foils, the metallic vinyls have the capacity to cover up wall imperfections.

Bathroom ceilings leave the homeowner a number of important options which can greatly enhance the entire bathroom design. Depending upon house location and roof line, the bathroom ceiling can be: normal-height, flat-surface construction; sloped or vaulted with wood, flexible wallcovering or painted wallboard surfaces; suspended illuminated panels along or in combination with decorative drop-in panels; or a skylight area, flat or angled to provide daytime lighting.

Paint is the number one ceiling finishing material in the bathroom where plaster or gypsum wallboard materials are used for the structural surface. Ex-

perts recommend a coat of undercoating and two coats of semigloss enamel for best results due to the high moisture levels present in the bathroom. This finish wears well, is easy to clean, and is resistant to moisture.

Higher-than-normal bathroom ceilings can be painted a darker color than walls if you wish to create the illusion of the ceiling being lower. Bathroom walls and ceilings painted in tones of beige, lemon, eggshell, white, pale green, sky blue, and petal pink always appear larger in size than bathrooms painted in the deep shades of blue, green, and brown.

When using wallcoverings on a ceiling, this area always should be hung before the walls. Materials should be applied across the shorter dimension of the room, starting on the less critical side, or where it will be least noticeable. In measuring for ceilings, be certain to allow ½ inch overlaps for all adjoining walls.

Luminous ceilings are becoming increasingly

popular in the bathroom as recent improvements in fluorescent tubes provide much truer "natural" lighting than possible before and a longer lamp life at a reduced energy cost.

Natural lighting can be a key element of the bathroom ceiling design by means of a skylight. Such units can be used even when the bathroom is located below an unfinished attic.

There are several brands and types of skylights, including some that can be opened for ventilation. One version is "curb-mounted," which raises it slightly above roof level, and the other fits cleanly into the roofing shingles.

Washable vinyl in a newspaper pattern adds an amusing touch to this bathroom. The white window shade and matching valance have crimson trimming to pick up the accents in the pictures and hand towels. Photo courtesy of the Window Shade Manufacturers Association

Linen Stripe 16 inch by 8 foot prefinished planks were used in this bathroom remodeling project. Linen Stripe has a washable plastic finish which resists hard wear, heat, moisture, and stains. Tongue-and-groove edges simplify installation with concealed clips and adhesive. Photo courtesy of Marlite

The antique elegance achieved in this simple remodeled bathroom flaunts a stained-glass window and crystal chandelier. The ceiling has washable, drop-in panels in a metal grid while the washable walls have a marblelike finish. Photo courtesy of Marlite

An authentic reproduction of Appalachian slate has been used for the tub wall, lavatory countertop, and side walls of this bathroom setting. The new decorative plastic laminate contrasts well with the dark paneling. Photo courtesy of Evans Products Co.

Floors

Bathroom floors are subjected to water and moisture and therefore should be surfaced with materials that resist water. Resilient flooring (in tile or roll form), ceramic tile, and carpeting are the flooring materials most commonly used in bathrooms.

Careful attention should be given to purchasing and installing resilient flooring. When the location is on or below grade level, you may choose from asphalt, vinyl-asbestos, rubber, and solid vinyl. In all applications, a waterproof adhesive is specified. Use of sheet materials is preferred by many homeowners. This material is the least susceptible to moisture seepage because sheet goods can be coved and installed with a minimum number of seams. (See *Kitchen Planning and Remodeling* for vinyl sheet floor covering installation instructions.)

Asphalt tile is the least expensive tile material and costs approximately one-third the installed price of rubber or vinyl tile. Vinyl-asbestos tile has a coating of clear plastic that wears well. This material is priced between asphalt and vinyl tile. Ceramic tile can be laid at grade or above grade level with waterproof grouting applied. When installing any type of tile, be sure to purchase several extra

Resilient floor tile can be installed over a concrete or wood subfloor. Waterproof adhesive should be used for all resilient materials.

pieces for possible future replacement. Patterns and glazes available change and often it is impossible to match colors a few years after installation.

Nylon and olefin (polypropylene) are the most commonly used types of carpeting for bathrooms. Both resist soil and moisture and are long-wearing. Carpets of olefin fiber are virtually stain-proof and provide the functional benefits of warmth, noise reduction and beauty. The fabric can be easily maintained because soil remains on the surface of the fiber and does not penetrate the mat.

In a small bathroom, a light-colored floor looks larger and more unbroken than a dark or patterned floor. Unless the bathroom is unusually large, it is better to avoid borders of a different color. The closer all the bathroom surfaces are to each other in color, the larger and more unified the room will appear. When selecting plumbing fixtures, manufacturers can provide you with color charts to help you determine compatible colors for room surfaces and accessories.

Plumbing Systems

When it comes to planning the plumbing for a new or remodeled bathroom, your best course of action is to rely on a competent plumbing contractor. Most builders and architects planning new home developments carefully review floor plans with their plumbing contractor, or even with a plumbing engineer, to determine the most economical arrangement. If you plan to move fixtures, always try to keep runs of hot water pipe as short as possible.

The basic "mechanical core" of your plumbing system is installed in the wall and floor of the room. It consists of vents, traps, waste lines and soil stacks, and hot and cold water supply lines. Basically, there are two types of plumbing systems—that which is totally fabricated at the site, and that which is prefabricated off-site, trucked to the job and dropped into position, often before the roof of the home is put in place.

Various types of prefabricated systems are available. One type is a core unit which combines a complete kitchen and bathroom in a single modular package. All fixtures and appliances are factory-installed and the total unit is set in place with a crane ready for hook-up to supply and waste piping. Another type of prefabricated system is the so-called "plumbing tree" which provides drain, waste, vent, and supply lines all tied together. This unit also is set in place before the roof goes on the home. It is engineered to the specific floor plan and is fabricated with materials to meet specific local building code requirements. Still another variation

A pressure-sensitive asbestos felt sheet system for installation of ceramic tile eliminates, in many cases, the need for mastic, thin-set mortar, or epoxy adhesive. The four-foot-square sheets may be used with glazed tile, ceramic mosaics, and quarry tile, and can be applied over plywood, concrete, existing ceramic tile, hardwood floors, or resilient flooring. Photo courtesy of American Olean

of the plumbing tree used in some areas of the country is a unit which provides a four-foot "half-wall" including horizontal piping only. The vertical plumbing is then installed at the job site to complete the installation.

Four major types of pipe are used in residential plumbing systems—copper, galvanized iron, cast iron, and plastic, the latter in two types, polyvinyl chloride (PVC) and arylonitrile butadine styrene (ABS). Regional and local building and plumbing codes detail where and when each type may be used. Some local codes do not permit plumbing by persons other than licensed contractors.

Although most plumbing systems are based upon national codes, your local building code concerning plumbing may vary from the code in an adjoining city or town. Therefore, it is wise to check the local code before making any major change. Generally speaking, your plumber will be most familiar with what you can and cannot do as specified by local codes.

According to the National Association of Home Builders, cast iron is the most widely used pipe for drain, waste, and vent systems. Plastic pipe is second in preference, followed by copper and galvanized iron. Copper is the material most often used for supply lines, followed by galvanized iron and plastic.

Lower weight and easier fabrication has caused many builders and plumbers to favor plastic piping

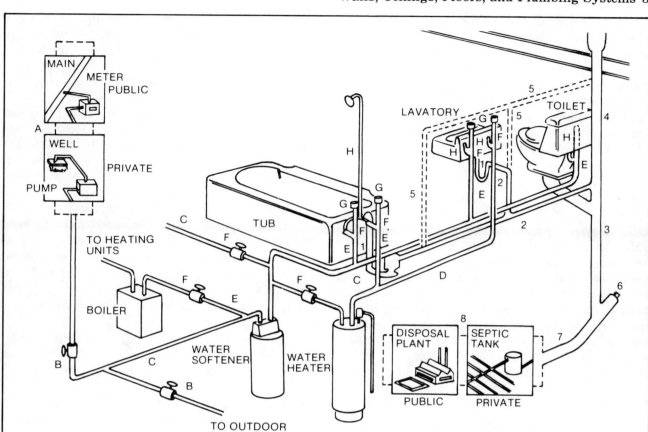

Major parts of the plumbing system: **Supply system parts:** *(A) Water source, public, or private. For our purpose it includes all piping up to the building. (B) Drain cock or shutoff valve. One is required at the low point of the system. (C) Cold-water main line (any line serving two or more fixtures). (D) Hot-water main line (any line serving two or more fixtures). (E) Branch line to fixture (any line, for cold or hot water, that serves one fixture only). (F) Shutoff valve, recommended for use in all branch lines and in main lines wherever a cutoff might be required. (G) Air chamber, recommended for any branch line terminating in a faucet. It helps eliminate chatter. (H) Fixture supply line. This is the portion of a branch line (above) that is installed when the fixture itself is installed and is adapted to its special requirements.* **Drainage system parts:** *(1) Fixture drain, the portion of a branch drain (below) adapted to the requirements of the particular fixture. Each drain must incorporate a trap (unless a trap is built into the fixture) that*

will hold water and seal the drain line against the escape of gases into the house. (2) Branch drain, a line between a fixture and a soil stack. (3) Soil stack, a vertical pipe that collects from the branch drain or drains. Every installation must have one **main** *stack, that is, a stack built of 3- or 4-inch pipe (depending on the building code), extending all the way through the roof. There may be a* **secondary** *stack or stacks, built of smaller pipe (usually 2-inch), either throughout or in the vent portion only. (4) Vent, upper portion of a soil stack, through which gases escape to the outside and air enters the stack. (5) Re-vent, a bypass for air between a branch drain and the vent portion of a stack. It is required by some codes. (6) Cleanout. One should be placed at every point where access may be needed to clear an obstruction (always at the foot of each stack). (7) Building drain. It receives waste from the stack or stacks and carries it to the final disposal. (8) Final disposal, either the public sewer or a private septic tank.*

for DWV (drain-waste-vent) systems. For example, identical plumbing trees for one installation show this variation in weights:

- cast iron weighing 156 pounds
- copper at 35 pounds
- plastic at 20 pounds

From the standpoint of time, it takes about one minute to make a joint in a 3-inch PVC stack, far quicker than with cast iron.

Residential plumbing systems, both prefabricated and site-fabricated, connect to city sewerage, sep-

tic tanks or cesspools for disposal. The most common city sewer system includes all drain lines, including rain water and sanitary, taking all disposable materials away from the property.

Septic tanks are watertight receptacles which receive the discharge of the drainage system. They are designed and constructed to retain solids, digest organic matter through a period of retention and allow the liquids to discharge into the soil outside of the tank through a system of open-joint piping or a seepage pit built to conform to the plumbing code.

Septic tanks are built of metal or cast concrete and require cleaning every two or three years on the average. However, these tanks should be inspected annually, preferably in the spring of the year.

A cesspool is a lined excavation in the ground which receives the discharge of the drainage system and is designed to retain the organic matter and solids while permitting the liquids to seep through the bottom and sides. Cesspools are usually constructed of hollow concrete block or stone.

Waste lines and soil stacks connect with the plumbing fixtures in the bathroom or lavatory, making it possible for waste to flow to the main disposal system of your home, the sewer or septic tank. The waste piping is smaller in diameter than the main soil pipe buried in your yard. Relocating waste lines and soil stacks in the bathroom when remodeling can be very expensive and in some instances virtually impossible. In homes with concrete slab flooring, for example, the waste lines and soil stacks are embedded in concrete and would have to be cut out if relocation of fixtures were desired. In homes with crawl space or sufficient area under the bathroom floor, these lines can be relocated, but even then it is expensive to do so.

The typical residential plumbing system consists of these basic components:

- Soil stack—a 3- or 4-inch pipe which runs vertically from the lowest point in the system to six or more inches above the roof line where it is flashed for protection from the weather. The stack may extend more than one story and when equipped with aerator fittings (for self-venting), a single stack can be used for waste and vent plumbing in multi-story buildings such as apartments. Two stacks can be tied together at the top above the highest fixture with only one stack extending through the roof line.
- Drain pipes—usually 1½ inches minimum to accommodate bathtubs, shower stalls, lavatories, and laundry trays. Also called "branches," these pipes are joined into the vertical soil stack. While lavatories can be adequately drained with 1½-inch branches, water closets require a minimum soil branch size of 3 inches, and both bathtubs and shower stalls are best served by 2-inch waste branches. It might also be noted that water closets should be located with a minimum of 15 inches of area from the center of the fixture to the wall or cabinets at each side. A minimum space of 24 inches should be allowed from the front rim of the water closet to the facing wall surface.
- Vent stacks—provide a flow of air to or from a drainage system and force a circulation of air within the system to protect trap seals from siphonage and back pressure. Vent stacks are usu-

ally 2 inches in diameter and run from the horizontal drain line at the base to an intersection in the vertical soil stack. This latter connection must be at least 6 inches above the overflow rim of the uppermost fixture served. Vent stacks continue through the roof line and may be no closer than 10 feet to a window, door opening, air intake, or ventilating shaft. The vents must be 10 feet above the ground level and 6 inches above the roof line. The vent must also be at least 3 feet in every direction from any lot line. Fixtures without vents can, under certain conditions, siphon water from the traps and allow potentially dangerous sewer gases to enter the room.

- Supply lines—typically ½-inch copper pipe with hot water line installed vertically a minimum of 6 inches to the left of cold water line when faucet side is viewed from the front. Lines from the outdoor meter to the water heater are generally ¾ to 1 inch in diameter.
- Traps—curved pipe or tubing shaped like the letters "S" or "P" which, when properly vented, produce a liquid seal which will prevent the back passage of air without materially affecting the flow of sewage or waste water through it. Approved connections are measured from the trap to vent along a horizontal line, except a water closet or bidet, which is measured to include the developed distance from the top of the floor flange to the inner edge of the vent.

Limits established for the distance between trap and vent in continuous waste and vent systems include the following for residential applications:

- 2'6" maximum for one fixture using 1¼" pipe (usually for lavatories)
- 3'6" maximum for bathtubs and laundry traps using 1½" pipe
- 5'0" maximum for shower stall or floor drain using 2" pipe
- 6'0" maximum for floor drain using 3" pipe
- 10'0" maximum for floor drain using 4" pipe

The maximum pitch on any trap arm is ¼ inch per foot.

It is well to check the available water pressure when installing an additional bathroom. One way to do this is to turn on several faucets in the house for a few minutes. If the pressure falls off noticeably, the outside water supply may be inadequate. Larger pipes may be needed to make up for it. Another factor to consider in remodeling or adding a bathroom is the size of your water heater and its recovery rate. The average 2½-bathroom house with an automatic washer and/or dishwasher requires at least a 50-gallon hot water tank, and a 60- or 72-gallon unit is recommended to insure adequate hot water for normal household use.

Bathrooms do not have to be small or look small any longer. Greenhouse windows, skylights, plants, and ceramic tile give this spacious master bathroom an open, natural appearance. The focal point is a combination whirlpool-bathtub. Photo courtesy of Kohler

Mirrored walls make a small bathroom seem larger. Soft fluorescent lighting and plant groups provide a bright, natural feeling in bathrooms without windows or a natural light source. Photo courtesy of Hedrich-Blessing

The colorful molding and wainscot treatment give this bathroom a delightful Early American look. The design is efficient and functional as well as attractive. Photo courtesy of American Standard.

This older bathroom was remodeled in Early American furnishings to enhance the room's strongest element, the large window above the radiator. Shutters were added to the window, and a pedestal lavatory replaced the original. Photo courtesy of American Olean Tile

A built-in tile bench above the radiant-heating unit doubles as a bench for basking under the sunlamp or a display area for potted plants. The floor is random-set green slate. Photo courtesy of American Olean Tile

The L-shaped cabinets blend well with the decor of this bathroom. The white countertop matches the cabinet doors, and the wood of the cabinets coordinates with the wall paneling. Photo courtesy of Kohler

A larger bathroom is possible by adding on to a present one. The enclosed bathtub in this bathroom is recessed from the rest of the room. A skylight and windows were added to allow sunshine to fill the room. Photo courtesy of Kohler

Even with limited space, an attractive bathroom is possible. This conventional bathroom floor plan is enhanced by the addition of the skylight above the bathtub. Photo courtesy of Eljer Plumbing

Today fixtures are available in a wide variety of styles, colors, and sizes. Here, green fixtures were selected to complement the attractive plant groupings. Photo courtesy of Gerber Plumbing Fixtures Corp.

Successful bathrooms are a combination of products and materials tastefully assembled to provide an attractive and functional setting. Pedestal lavatories and footed bathtubs are becoming popular again. Nature is incorporated in this bathroom by means of the plants and flowers. Photo courtesy of Armstrong Cork Co.

Japanese architecture continues to influence bathroom design in America. This serene bathroom features the natural textures of bamboo, quarry tile, and wood. The bathtub wall and countertop are covered with plastic laminate in a marble pattern. Photo courtesy of Kohler.

Mirrored walls and glass shelving make this small bathroom appear more spacious. The hand-held shower head adds to the functional aspect of this attractive bathroom. Photo courtesy of Hedrich-Blessing

This handsome bathroom is an excellent example of how dark colors can be used to make an attractive bathroom. The wooden beams and dark print wallpaper contrast nicely with the white ceramic tile. Photo courtesy of Eljer

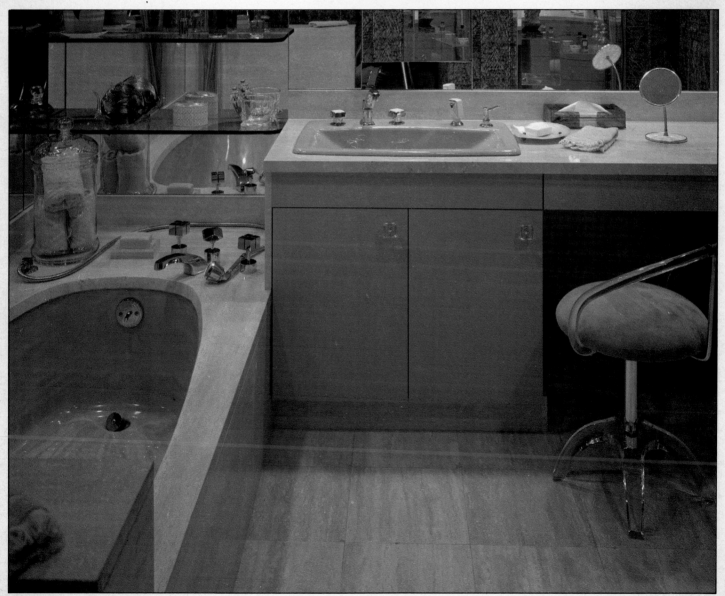

The ever-popular Early American look is practical as well as attractive. This remodeled bath features textured paneling in wormy chestnut pattern, durable plastic laminate countertop, and self-rimming lavatory bowls. Photo courtesy of Marlite

This bathroom was added when the homeowner decided to finish off the attic. The long, narrow room leads directly to the shower and tub area. The large skylight supplies more than enough light during the day. Photo courtesy of Kohler

The bathtub and shower are separate to add to the functional aspect of this bathroom. The luminous ceiling is framed in the same material as the mirrors. Photo courtesy of Formica

Decorative hardware and colorful knickknacks enhance this Early American compartmented bathroom. Cabinets are natural wood with a plastic laminate countertop that matches the bathtub. Photo courtesy of Ajax Hardware

This decorator lavatory bowl is a vitreous china unit with a lifetime pattern. Decorator bowls enhance any bathroom design. Both self-rimming and under-counter types are available. Photo courtesy of Gerber Plumbing Fixtures Corp.

Prefinished tile panels and ceramic tile products are available to make beautiful bathtub-shower areas like this relatively simple to build. The tile surface is easy to clean with a damp cloth. Photo courtesy of Marlite

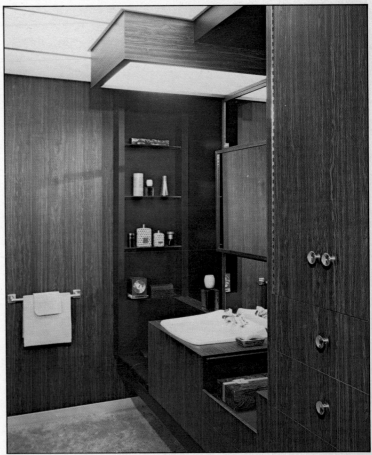

This bathroom features a six-foot wardrobe closet with folding doors, built-in drawers, toiletry case, lavatory, and cushioned seat that can be closed off from the rest of the bathroom. All cabinetwork is finished in Formica and the plumbing fixtures are by Eljer

Since the bathroom is often the smallest room in the house, adequate storage is at a premium. A built-in linen closet with shelving and drawers and a vanity with extra drawers can solve storage problems in the bathroom. Photo courtesy of Nutone

Separate dressing and grooming areas for him and for her are among the features of this spacious bathroom. The sunken bathtub is flanked by a compartmented water closet and shower area. In keeping with contemporary master bathroom design, an exercise area is in the center of the room. Photo courtesy of American Olean Tile

Cedar planks and ceramic tile lend a rough, natural look to this bathroom. Natural materials require little maintenance and are easy to clean. Photo courtesy of Hedrich-Blessing

Creative use of unfinished attic space resulted in this luxurious master bathroom. The large skylight above the bathtub and the marble paneling on the walls and around the tub give the room a light, clean appearance. Photo courtesy of Kohler

Plastic laminates in floral and woodgrain patterns highlight the decor of this bathroom. The separate shower and tub areas add to the functional aspect. Photo courtesy of Formica

Lighting for the Bathroom

Regardless of size or shape, every bathroom usually needs two types of lighting—general and directed. In a very small bathroom or powder room, a single light in the ceiling or above the mirror or medicine cabinet may provide sufficient general and directed lighting, but mirror sidelights are also recommended. Lighting engineers recommend 30 footcandles of illumination for the bathroom. This is the equivalent of 3.5 to 4 watts of incandescent lighting per square foot of floor area, or 1.5 to 2 watts of fluorescent lighting.

The greatest need for directed lighting in the bathroom is for shaving and makeup. A ceiling fixture above the mirror and a light fixture on each side of the mirror will illuminate the face without shadows. All three fixtures are usually wired to and controlled by one wall switch. Combination overhead lighting units complete with exhaust fans and heater elements are also available. These units often are controlled by a wall timer, especially the fan and heater functions.

Another popular ceiling treatment is the wall-to-wall or large-area luminous ceiling with fluorescent tubes installed above removable plastic panels suspended in a metal or wood ceiling grid. A more even distribution of light throughout the room is provided.

Incandescent lamps are generally preferred for use in areas where women apply makeup as this type of illumination most closely resembles sunlight. Always choose white bulbs for bathroom use, as tinted bulbs or shades distort colors. When one or more lavatory basins are installed in a vanity countertop more than four feet wide, several 75-watt incandescent bulbs or two rows of fluorescent tubes above the mirror in a soffit at least 15 inches from front to back will give even, adequate illumination.

Vapor-proof fixtures are recommended for use in tub and shower areas. Electrical outlets should be carefully placed in the bathroom to accommodate the use of an electric razor, hair dryers, electric comb, toothbrush, etc. These outlets, of course, should be grounded and should not be placed near the bathtub for safety's sake.

Soffit lighting is enhanced by an L-shaped mirror arrangement in this bathroom, which incorporates the three most used bathroom materials—wood, ceramic tile, and decorative plastic laminate. Photo courtesy of American Olean

Here are some basic "rules of lighting" as recommended by General Electric:
- Lighting small mirrors: Use three fixtures, wired to one switch.

Incandescent. The ceiling unit should be centered over the front edge of the lavatory bowl or countertop. The fixture should be a minimum 12-inch diameter with two 60-watt bulbs. Wall brackets should be centered on the mirror, 30 inches apart and 60 inches above the floor. At minimum, a 6-inch diameter should have one 75-watt each,

Translucent plastic panels conceal four 40-watt fluorescent tubes in this wood-framed, luminous ceiling. The plastic panels are easily removed and may be washed in the bathtub or shower. Carriage lamps double as night lights. It would have been better to place the mirror 8 inches above the counter to prevent splash marks.

Light is directed onto the washbasin by flanking lamps, rather than reflecting from the mirror. Photo courtesy of Eljer Plumbingware

spaced 16 to 24 inches apart. Pendants of equal or greater diameter should be similarly spaced.

Fluorescent. Use deluxe warm white tubes with trigger start ballasts, located and wired to one switch. Ceiling fluorescents should be two- to four-tube units (20 watt) 24 inches in length and shielded. Fluorescent 20-watt wall-bracket units should flank the mirror with the center of the tube located 60 inches above the floor.

- Lighting large mirrors: Mirrors 36 inches or greater in width should be illuminated with a double row of deluxe warm white (30-watt, 36 inch; or 40-watt, 48 inch) fluorescent tubes in a recessed fixture or custom built into a soffit. Recommended soffit dimensions: 16 inches front to back; 8 inches deep; full length of counter.
- Theatrical effect: Exposed-lamp fixtures across the top and sides of a mirror should include four to six lamps per fixture. Decorative 15-watt or 25-watt bulbs are recommended. Side strips should be 30 inches apart.

Lighting in separate compartments of the bathroom should be a minimum one 75-watt, R-30 type unit recessed in the ceiling, or an 8-inch diameter 100-watt surface mounted fixture or wall bracket. Fixtures used in the shower or tub area should be recessed and use the vapor-proof type 75- or 100-watt, with a switch outside of shower area. A bathroom night-light can be either a 15-watt switched wall bracket or plug-in type units with 4- or 7-watt bulb. Sunlamps should be equipped with a timing device. Infrared heatlamps should be used in U/L-approved fixtures.

Light from the flower-petal lamp catches the gleam of smooth tile in this sleek, compact design. Photo courtesy of American Olean Tile

Twin bathtubs and pedestal lavatories are featured in this elaborate multilevel bathroom. A conventional single bath sunk into a tile platform can be equally spectac-ular for persons with smaller bathrooms. Ceramic tile is used throughout. Photo courtesy of Tile Council of America

Bathtubs and Surrounds

Today's bathtub has come a long way from the wooden or galvanized tub originally brought from the side porch to the center of the kitchen on Saturday night. Instead of the Spartan dunking ritual, we now have bathtubs designed for comfort and relaxation.

Color is making the traditional white tub a fixture of the past, just as modern design is adding an elegance never found in the bathroom before. Major manufacturers now produce a great selection of bathtub styles, sizes and shapes to meet almost every conceivable bathroom plan.

- The rectangular tub—a standby for better than a half century, ranges from 4 to 6 feet in length, is just under 3 feet in width and is 12 to 16 inches high. Sloping backs, body-contour designs, slip-resistant bottoms and safety-grip handles are among the latest features. Many units have a convenient integral seat that can easily double as a handy tub-side shelf for soaps and toiletries.

- The square tub—is typically 31 to 48 inches long, 42 to 49 inches wide and 12 to 16 inches high. This fixture, installed in a recessed area or corner, can solve the problem of limited space. The square tub doubles very well as a shower receptor.

- The sunken tub—more popular each year as greater emphasis is placed on good bathroom design. This type of installation can be either a custom-design fixture created with ceramic tile, or a factory-made fixture produced for "sinking" in the floor or a raised platform. One manufacturer's version of the sunken bath is a steeping model which measures 15⅛ inches deep, nearly 6½ inches deeper than most conventional tubs. With arm rests incorporated into the interior design of the tub, this model provides a high degree of reclining comfort. Another steeping-type tub on the market has a 55 x 37 inch interior to accommodate two persons, side by side. This unit fits into a standard 5-foot width area and uses standard fittings.

Most bathtubs on the market are manufactured from one of three materials—molded cast iron with a porcelain enamel surface; formed steel with a porcelain enamel surface; or fiberglass.

The cast iron tub dates back to 1870, while enameling can be traced to the ancient Egyptians and Assyrians. These tubs are the heaviest, weighing from 200 to 500 pounds, with a 1/16-inch (approximate) coating of porcelain. They are also the least susceptible to damage.

Formed steel tubs weigh but 100 pounds and thus are generally preferred for remodeling purposes as well as for use on upper floors of homes and apartments. These units feature the same porcelain enamel finish as cast iron, but are less costly. Two types are manufactured: one-piece with integral apron (front); and two-piece with a separate apron which is welded into place before the enameling process. The obvious welded seam may be offensive to some buyers. Manufacturers offer a sound-deadening coating for both styles of formed steel tubs and the reasonable cost is usually justified by the resulting reduction of shower noise.

Fiberglass tubs are the newest development, with the units in widespread use since around 1968. Lightweight yet durable, these units come in a wide range of colors and in many instances incorporate surrounding panels which form a tub-shower combination. Oval-shape fiberglass tub designs are

In the price range of the traditional bathtub is this soaking bath that requires the same floor space as a shower stall and can be installed in tandem with a shower when space permits. The bath is of one-piece molded fiberglass with a semicircular seat near the bottom. Photo courtesy of American-Standard

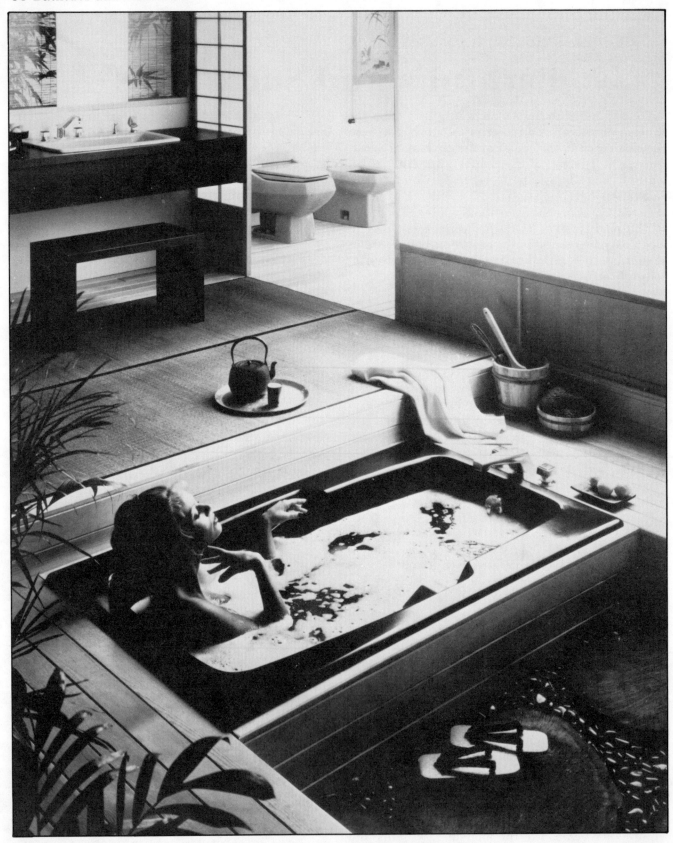

This steeping bath is 20 inches deep, almost six inches more than most five-foot bathtubs, and affords deep-down soaking. A three-foot width and gently sloping back provide added comfort. Safety features include grip handles and a slip-resistant bottom. This tub has a no-apron design for installation in a corner, island, or peninsula setting, or in a recess, virtually at any level. The tub comes in 13 colors. Photo courtesy of Kohler

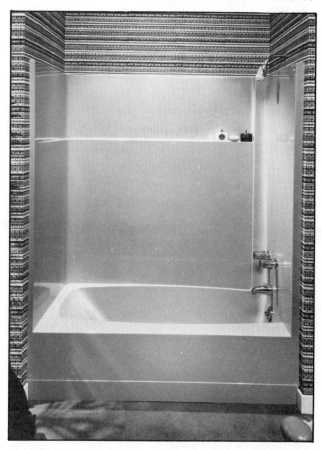

This sunken bathtub combines stretch-out comfort and safety. Six feet long and three feet wide, this bath has a gently sloping back for reclining ease, safety-grip rails, and slip-resistant bottom. It can be installed as a sunken tub with the rim flush with the floor, or it can be set at any height with one, two, three, or all four sides exposed and faced with decorative plastic laminate or other material. Photo courtesy of Kohler

The figure-fitting backrest of this fiberglass tub and surround supports the user's lumbar area. The wide front apron holds accessories and doubles as a grooming seat. Shoulder-high shelf holds shower aids. The unit is available in several colors. Photo courtesy of American-Standard

Only ground preparation and an electrical connection are required to make this preplumbed spa fully operational. The spa can accommodate between 5 and 7 people. The unit can be used in the bathroom or in the yard and can be filled with a garden hose. Photo courtesy of Jacuzzi

Victorian fixtures are making a comeback. Commonly found in many turn-of-the-century homes, footed tubs and pedestal lavatories are now available at some bathroom remodeling stores. Photo courtesy of Tile Council of America

common with the 5-foot length being the most popular size. These molded, one-piece units can incorporate arm rests, integral seats, and shelves. They are kept clean with a sponge or cloth and liquid detergent. Users are cautioned to use only manufacturer-approved cleaners for this purpose.

Hand in hand with the yearly improvements made in manufacturing fiberglass tubs has come the development of whirlpool baths and spas designed to dramatically change the Spartan bathing ritual to a luxurious happening.

From their start as hydrotherapy equipment in hospitals and athletic training rooms, whirlpool baths are making their way into private homes at an astonishing rate. In warm-weather areas, the units are installed outdoors where circular, square, oval and other shapes are large enough to accommodate from two to over a half dozen persons simultaneously.

The values of hydrotherapy can be traced to the ancient Egyptians and Greeks and still hold true for persons of all ages. Hydro-massage helps relieve the pain of those suffering from bursitis, arthritis, aching back and sore muscles.

Some whirlpool spas on the market are sold as complete package units with no extra fittings to purchase. Others permit a selection of conventional faucets and controls.

A nostalgic blend of yesterday and today, this footed tub is six feet long and 37½ inches wide with an enameled interior bonded to cast iron, and a smooth, rolled rim. The tub comes in antique red, black, and white. Ball and claw feet match antique-style faucets of chromium or gold electroplate, either brushed or polished. Photo courtesy of Kohler

New whirlpool baths in fiberglass and durable enameled cast iron come in a wide range of decorator colors. They can be installed in the floor, raised on a platform, as an island, in a corner, or in a peninsular setting. Some also are available with a snap-on skirt for free-standing applications.

Interior configurations of the whirlpool baths permit the bather or bathers to recline comfortably with the top edge of the tub serving as head rest.

The number of hydrojets varies from model to model as does their placement. Eljer's Continental AquaSpa system has six flush-mounted hydrojets, each omnidirectional and strategically placed to reach the lower back and spine, upper back and neck, arms and shoulder, legs and feet. Kohler's steeping bath whirlpool is 20 inches deep (6 inches more than standard tubs) and has four jets. Jacuzzi Whirlpool Bath Inc. offers units fully plumbed in the bath itself, complete with a master console incorporating the controls for silent air induction system, drain and vented overflow, water valve spill spout, and venturi inlets. Jacuzzi also offers among its other models a deep soaking unit that is standard shower size and has a full integrated wall surround.

This oversized bathtub is made of fiberglass-reinforced polyester. The unit is big enough for two persons and has a built-in seat which doubles as an accessory holder.

The tub comes in six colors. Photo courtesy of American-Standard

One of the biggest bathtubs on the market is this 5½ x 7 foot fiberglass bathing oval. It can be sunk into a floor or

raised on a platform and is available with dual showers and dual water controls. Photo courtesy of Kohler

Silver and white are the dominant colors in this master bathroom with foil-covered walls and raised bathing-relaxing platform. The off-the-floor built-in vanity is finished in square-edged decorative plastic laminate. Photo courtesy of Universal-Rundle

Less than an hour's time is required to install a glazed ceramic tile bathtub surround. The wainscot-height, 49-square-foot package consists of eight pregrouted sheets of tile, with trim attached, and two internal cove corner strips which allow for a ⅜-inch variation in size of the tub recess. The system can be installed over properly sealed gypsum wallboard, concrete masonry, plywood, or gypsum plaster. It's waterproof, and highly stain- and mildew-resistant. The silicone rubber used in factory grouting is also used for perimeter grouting and sealing at installation time. The only cutting required is for pipe holes and for tub "legs." Photo courtesy of American-Standard

Shower Stalls and Doors

Shower stalls can be custom fabricated during the construction of a new bathroom or they can be purchased in prefabricated form from various manufacturers in a wide range of sizes and styles. All shower stalls require care and attention during installation to prevent possible leakage which can rot the shower underlayment and surrounding framework.

Factory-made, one-piece units, are obviously the quickest and easiest to install. However, remodeling often requires three-piece or four-piece units which can be moved into an existing area via a doorway which would not be big enough to permit passage of a one-piece, fully assembled unit.

Gel-coated fiberglass bath-showers are offered in colors to coordinate with lavatories and water closets. The units often incorporate built-in seats for sit-down showering, and corner ledges for soaps and toiletries, built-in grab bars and nonslip bases.

Another feature of the one-piece tub-shower combination is the smooth, easy-to-maintain wall surface which eliminates 50 square feet or more of wallboard and tile or panels. The unbroken surface prevents possible leaks and there are no joints or grout lines to keep clean.

Fiberglass shower stalls range in size from 32 x 32 to 53½ x 38¾ inches. Heights range from 75 to 90 inches. The units may be fitted with rod and shower curtain or conventional shower doors. Metal shower stalls finished with baked enamel or vitreous porcelain enamel also are widely used in remodeling. The units are designed so that all joints between panels are flanged to interlock with one another for easy waterproofing. Floors of these units are precast to provide floor, threshold and curb. Reinforced plastic or precast terrazzo are generally used.

Clay tile is most often used for custom-installed shower stalls, but other waterproofed surfacing materials are also satisfactory. Careful attention should be given to waterproofing joints.

Standard sizes range from 32 x 32 to 40 x 40 inches. Standard trim includes brass mixing valves, shower head, soap dish, vinyl curtain, and curtain rings. Shower doors are generally optional. While the custom shower can be any desired size, standard floor receptors for this purpose come in such dimensions as 32 x 32, 36 x 36, 48 x 32, 54 x 33 and 40 x 40-inch corner models. Likewise, the floor may be fabricated of clay tile with a subsurface shower pan

Shower receptors such as this 34 x 48-inch model are often used in combination with ceramic tile in creating custom shower stalls. The premolded units eliminate the need for bulky lead pans. Photo courtesy of American-Standard

made of sheet lead, copper, or waterproof and damp-proof membrane formed to the desired size and shape. The membrane material is a lamination of heavy paper and asphalt reinforced with glass fibers and costs considerably less than sheet lead or copper.

When planning a custom-designed shower, it is well to consult with your contractor or plumber to make sure that construction will conform with local building and sanitation codes.

Depending upon the final design of the shower stall, it may require a waterproof light fixture, or it may be lighted by fixtures elsewhere in the room.

These folding shower doors are rigid bypassing units that also fold by simply unhooking the outside towel bar and inside grab bar. The design permits both doors to *fold into small stacks at either end for complete tub-shower access. The doors come in a wide range of decorator colors. Photo courtesy of Tub-Master Corp.*

Standard location of grab bars is 48 inches above the floor, while soap dishes should be recessed 54 inches from the floor. Shower head location varies from 60 to 66 inches from the floor and may incorporate a personal shower head for localized bathing and simplified cleanup. Single-handle mixing valves are preferred in the shower for added safety in dialing the desired water temperature. Use of an exhaust fan in the ceiling of the shower will remove steam and some moisture.

Shower Enclosures

Bath enclosures, shower enclosures and shower doors are manufactured in two basic types—rigid aluminum framed units, and flexible folding models. Both styles are offered in standard sizes and can be ordered in custom sizes as well.

Rigid enclosures vary in size from the single-door swing model to the by-passing double-door type used with bathtubs. Frames are of extruded aluminum while panels are tempered glass or 3/16-inch plastic in a variety of colors. The sliding units operate on nylon rollers and feature self-draining tracks. Width-wide handles on many units may be used for towel racks.

The flexible folding shower door and enclosure usually have the same anodized silver or gold aluminum frame as the rigid-type unit and provide nearly full access to the tub or shower when folded back to a mere 8 to 10 inches. This type of enclosure is made of high impact polystyrene, which will not shatter and is easy to maintain. Folding units are offered in a wide range of colors and decorator designs and can be installed in about 30 minutes. Available models in many instances are keyed to the catalog number of major manufacturers of bathtubs and showers to enable a perfect fit.

Before-and-after views illustrate the see-through mirror type bathtub enclosure. Available in shower stall and tub models, the door is transparent on one side and a mirrored surface on the other. The unit offers privacy for the bather without obstructing vision. The glass is made to the same specification as automobile windows and is four to six times stronger than ordinary glass. The hardware is gold anodized aluminum. Photo courtesy of Sierracin/Agalite Bronson

Open-area garden-type showers can be created with a wide selection of glazed and unglazed wall tile and ceramics. Note the lowered dressing table area with hamper doubling as seat. Photo courtesy of Franciscan Hermosa

Molded shower floors are available in various sizes and are manufactured with nonporous and nonslip surfaces. The one-piece units can be installed faster and at a lower cost than the custom lead pans often used in the construction of ceramic tile showers.

Lavatories

The lavatory (or bathroom sink) offers the greatest possible selection when it comes to designing a new bathroom or remodeling an existing one. There are many styles, shapes and sizes offered in a choice of vitreous china, cast iron, formed steel and plastic. In determining your needs, it is wise to first select the specific type of lavatory from the six basic styles offered:

- Flush-mount—a unit which requires a metal ring or frame to hold it in place in the plastic laminate or tile countertop. One problem with this type of installation is keeping the rim joint clean.
- Self-rimming—a style which eliminates the metal framing rim as it rests on the countertop, overlapping the mounting hole.
- Under-the-counter—this unit is secured under the surface of the countertop by means of metal fasteners. The countertop opening corresponds to the shape of the bowl. These tops are usually plastic laminate, marble or a simulated "synthetic" marble. There are problems in keeping the underside clean, especially at the joint line.
- Integral lavatory-countertop—again, usually of synthetic marble or plastic, the one-piece units are seamless and easily cleaned. The entire unit rests on the cabinet framework and has predrilled holes for fittings.

- Wall-hung—the conventional unit known to most persons. This type is secured to the wall, juts out from it, leaves plumbing pipes exposed and provides no storage. It is the least expensive and requires the least space.
- Pedestal—reflecting the continental look being found in many new homes across the country. Sculptured in colorful vitreous china, these units stand 32 to 33 inches high, have concealed wall hangers for added stability, and conceal supply lines and trap in the pedestal. Various-shaped ledges provide ample space for essentials and the bowls range to 24 inches in width with anti-splash rims.

Lavatory shapes include rectangular, round, oval, shell designs, angles, swirls and triangular. Some units are designed for placement of the lavatory fittings on the bowl rim while others require installation of fittings in the surrounding countertop area.

Oval lavatory basins measure from 17 to 19 inches across the front and 14 to 16 inches front to back. Some designs have extra deep bowls for doing hand laundry and are not apt to cause splashing. Being rounded, they clean somewhat faster than fixtures with corners.

Circular lavatory basins are 18 to 19 inches in top diameter and approximately 13 inches bottom dia-

Offered in 12 colors, this lightweight plastic lavatory is chip-free, stain-resistant, and rustproof. It comes with 4 or 8 inch centers, measures 20 x 17 inches and has a depth of 6⅛ inches. Photo courtesy of American-Standard

A concealed front overflow is a feature of this 19 x 16-inch oval bowl. Designed for undercounter installation, the bowl is available in white and some decorator colors. Photo courtesy of Briggs

meter by 12 inches deep. Designed for installation in a 21-inch or wider countertop, some of these fixtures have concealed front overflows and anti-splash rims.

Triangular units come in dimensions such as 11 x 11, 16 x 16, 17 x 17 and 18 x 18 inches for use in corners or rooms where space is at a real premium. These units have a back ledge which provides space for soap and a water tumbler. Projection into the room is approximately 4 inches greater than the triangular edge dimension.

Specialty lavatories available from national manufacturers include "his" and "her" shampoo and grooming centers incorporating built-in spray arms and swing-away faucet spouts. One "her" version doubles as a miniature bathtub for bathing the baby.

Standard height for installation of lavatories is 31 inches from the floor to the top of the basin rim,

but units can be installed from 34 to 38 inches off the floor if they are to be used by adults only. An 8-inch space is recommended between the top of the lavatory and the bottom of the mirror or medicine cabinet installed above.

When two lavatory basins are to be used in the same countertop, a mimimum of 12 inches should be provided between adjoining fixture edges. For more elbow room when two people use adjoining basins, a 20-inch space between fixture edges is more satisfactory if space permits. The lavatory should be no closer than 6 to 8 inches from the side edge of the countertop to provide a small support ledge and prevent splashing on the floor. Location of basins at extreme ends of an L-shaped countertop is one method of providing for ample elbow room. The distance from the front of lavatories to the opposite wall or fixture on it should be a minimum of 20 inches.

A front self-draining soap rest is conveniently located below the lavatory rim of this vitreous china fixture. Also featured is a hidden overflow drain. Photo courtesy of Borg-Warner Plumbing Products

Designed for cramped bathrooms and powder rooms, this lavatory measures only 21 x 13 inches and can be used in a countertop as narrow as 15 inches from front to back. Photo courtesy of Kohler

This self-rimming lavatory is a vitreous china fixture with sculptured basin. The unit is 21 x 19 inches. Photo courtesy of Kohler

Just 18 inches in diameter, this self-rimming stainless steel lavatory has a satin finish bowl, brass outlets and is installed here with acrylic handled fittings. Photo courtesy of American-Standard

This powder room ensemble includes provincial vanity cabinet, cultured marble one-piece lavatory, gold-tone faucet and drain assembly, and matching toilet flush handle. Photo courtesy of Borg-Warner Plumbing Products

Designated the Man's Lav by Kohler, this 28 x 19-inch cast iron fixture has built-in dispenser for soap or lotion and spray shampoo fitting in addition to conventional water controls and faucet. The self-rimming lavatory is installed here in a plastic laminate countertop. Photo courtesy of Kohler

Designer lavatory bowls for bath or powder room feature a lifetime pattern for an unusual decorative effect. The pattern may be in black or gold, and the bowl may be self-rimming or under-the-counter style. Standard size is 19 x 16 inches. Photo courtesy of Gerber

Pedestal lavatories, popular in Europe and once used in the United States, are making a comeback. This model is 44 inches wide and offers as much surface space as many countertop and slab lavatories. The pedestal hides the trap and drain lines. Smaller-space 26- and 31-inch units are also available. Photo courtesy of Eljer Plumbingware

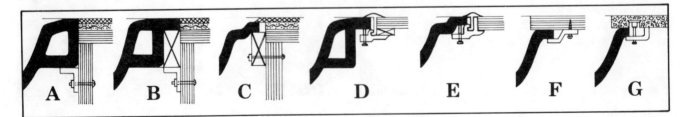

Recessing a lavatory can be accomplished by various means depending upon the type of countertop selected. Diagrams A, B, and C show lavatory bowls joined with ceramic tile countertops; D, E, and F are set in decorative plastic laminate; G is set in marble.

Bathroom Vanities and Countertops

Bathroom vanities add the appeal of fine furniture to bath and powder room settings and can be arranged in a virtually endless variety of combinations. Stock and custom units are offered with or without countertops and basins, affording the purchaser a wide degree of design flexibility.

While most bathroom installations include a bowl unit, combinations may be formed without a bowl unit for installation in dressing room, bedroom, hallway or other area of the home. Most units are modular in size to simplify planning and installation, but for rooms with odd dimensions, an exact fit can be accomplished with filler strips.

Standard cabinet units are available in widths of 12, 15, 18, 21, 24, 30, 36 and 48 inches. Front-to-wall dimension varies from 17 to 21 inches while the standard height is 29½ inches, minus top. Many units include a 4-inch kick space. Vanity bases are manufactured with one, two or more doors and are available with drawers right, left or flanking the doors. Additional arrangements are possible through custom arrangement. Drawers are available in both wood and plastic molded design while hardware, including knobs, pulls and self-closing hinges, is styled to give the desired effect.

Among the most popular styles of vanities are Early American, Spanish, Mediterranean, White & Gold, Provincial, and Contemporary. Nearly all feature carved doors or fronts reflecting the skill of cabinetmakers. Aside from natural wood, today's vanities are manufactured in a wide range of decorative plastic laminates which require virtually no maintenance. This durable material comes in solid colors, decorative patterns, and rich wood grains.

Countertops

Bathroom countertops are generally restricted to areas where decorator-style vanities are used, but in some cases the tops are also used for shelf-style installations, surrounds of tubs, and other areas where visible storage and utility are desired. Three types of materials are basic to most installations— decorative high-pressure plastic laminate (such as the well-known Formica), ceramic tile, and marble or synthetic marble. Plastic laminates are dominant throughout the United States, but in some regional areas tile is very popular.

Manufacturers of decorative plastic laminates recommend their 1/16 inch-thick material for all horizontal applications and caution that their 1/32 inch material should be confined to vertical applications such as walls and cabinet fronts. Plastic laminates open a wide range of design opportunities to those planning a new or remodeled bathroom. They come in literally hundreds of colors, patterns and wood grains, as well as new "leather" and "slate" three-dimensional textures.

Countertop fabricators use two terms to identify the types of bathroom countertops they offer: self-edged and postformed. The first term designates flat tops with a square front and a separate edging of the same material. The backsplash is again a

Federal oak, once so common in residential ice boxes, is used for this bathroom or powder room vanity. Oak paneling and decorative plastic laminate countertop complement this setting. Photo courtesy of Haas Cabinet Co.

Deep relief Spanish doors in oak or walnut set the style for this vanity. Bases are modular and available in two-door units of 24, 30, and 36 inches; the 36-inch unit is available in a 3-door unit with three hidden drawers right or left behind the third door. Photo courtesy of Formco

Color-fast white finish on this vanity is protected by a clear acrylic finish to prevent yellowing. Nontarnish gold edging and scrollwork are triple-sealed against flaking, chipping, and fading. Durable plastic laminate countertops in gold color were used in this master bedroom. Photo courtesy of NuTone

This vanity has a solid furniture front and a core stock with hardwood oak veneer face and back. All parts are machined for blind mortise and tenon, or dadoed and sanded for fit, then glued and pinned together. Photo courtesy of Connor

Molded louvered-style doors and washable vinyl interior simplify day-to-day maintenance of this vanity and matching wall cabinets. Units are offered in white walnut and cherry finish. Photo courtesy of Formco

separate piece with a square inside corner. Post-formed plastic laminate countertops are made of a single piece of the material, formed to provide a flat surface with rounded front edge and curved backsplash. This type surface has no joints to collect dirt or moisture and is easy to maintain.

Ceramic tile is available in a wealth of colors, sizes, and types for countertop installations as well as for walls, floors, showers and other areas of the bathroom. This hardy material is installed at the site, atop a specially prepared base stock affixed to the prefabricated vanity unit.

Among the most popular ceramic tile countertops are:

- Glazed tile—offered in hundreds of colors, has a smooth finish, and is impervious to heat, grease, spots and spills.
- Crystalline and scored tile—has a textured surface, usually gives the appearance of smaller tile as opposed to conventional 4¼ inch tiles. This type can also be used on floors and walls.
- Mosaics—solid and textured colors and forms a smooth dense surface. Many distinctive patterns are available.
- Quarry tile—unglazed, exceptionally rugged and is usually used for floors. Available primarily in "earthy" tones.
- Decorated tile—used primarily for "spot" applications in glazed surfaces to create a focal point. Hundreds of designs are available.

Manufactured bathroom vanity cabinets provide for numerous layout arrangements including this one-wall design. The dressing table area has its own immediate storage drawers, yet is separated from the washbowl area by a handy linen closet. Matching wall cabinets above the bowl are used for medicines. Photo courtesy of NuTone

Marble and synthetic marble countertops, installed as single-piece slabs, are resistant to scratches, mars, and stains, and are easily maintained.

DuPont's Corian is manufactured in white and two marble pattern colors. The nonporous material can be worked much like wood and can be fabricated with power tools. Standard sheets are offered in three thicknesses—¼ inch in 30 inch width and in lengths of 57, 72 and 98 inches; ½ and ¾ inch in 25 or 30-inch width, and in lengths of 98 and 121 inches.

Installation of a plastic laminate countertop has become a popular do-it-yourself bathroom remodeling project for many homeowners. Such installations call for high-pressure plastic lamination, bonded to particleboard and sold under such names as Formica, WilsonArt, Textolite, Micarta, Consoweld, Pionite, Melamite, Exxon Nevamar and Lamin-Art.

You can purchase the plastic surface and the particleboard substrate separately, and bond them yourself. But the bonding job must be perfect or it will delaminate. It may be better to buy an already-bonded "countertop blank" available in lengths up to 12 feet. You can cut it to size, and with a router you can carefully cut a hole for the lavatory bowl.

If you buy the blank, it will already be built up to the proper 1½" height, the front will be edged, and it will have a 5-inch backsplash. These are usually available at home centers.

If you are going to do it all yourself, buy ¾" particleboard 25 inches deep and as long as you need.

Specify industrial grade, not floor underlayment grade, and get a water-based contact adhesive for the bonding. Directions will be on the can. The plastic laminate itself comes in hundreds of colors and woodgrains, including metallics, slates and marble patterns. You will have to edge it, either with the same material or with a plastic or metal T-moulding which hammers into place in a precut groove. Or you may choose to "square" edge the entire surface much as a modern desktop.

Some manufacturers now offer countertop kits with everything properly sized except for length, and substrate. Be sure to get enough substrate to build it up along the perimeter to 1½ inches.

There are two ways to attach the counter to the base cabinet:

- Use panel mastic; run a ribbon of panel mastic the full length of the floor cabinet front and back. Position the top carefully on the glued area and set the countertop down in place.
- Use wood screws to go from the floor cabinet up into the counter wherever possible. If your vanity cabinet has triangular-shaped pieces in the corners, this would be the best place to use screws.

Caulking should be used along the crevice between the wall and edge of the countertop backsplash to waterproof the area. Also keep in mind that if the countertop is to fit between two walls, a 36 inch top will not fit perfectly in a 36 inch space between the two walls. Allow ¼ to ¾ inch for fitting it in.

Water Closets and Bidets

Considerable design improvements have been made in recent years in the construction of toilets (or water closets). These units are not all alike—some work better than others, some are quieter than others and some are more attractive than others. Plumbing engineers for many years have been trying to design a toilet with completely noiseless flushing action, but to date none have succeeded. However, the degree of noise is reduced substantially as the toilets range from the lowest-priced "washdown" model to the highest-priced "siphon action."

Most residential toilets consist of a bowl and a tank, with the tank providing sufficient water storage to create a proper flushing action in the bowl. While most toilets are floor mounted, wall-hung units are available to provide for easier floor maintenance. Water closets are offered in four basic models, each distinguished by its different flushing action:

- The washdown is the noisiest and least efficient. No longer acceptable in many areas, this unit is flushed by a simple wash-out action and tends to clog more easily than other models. Another disadvantage is that much of the bowl area is not covered by water and is therefore subject to fouling, staining, and contamination. Most major manufacturers have removed this type of water closet from their lines.
- The reverse trap units are less noisy than washdown models and are the least expensive of the siphon-action toilets. Similar in appearance to better siphon jet action toilets, these units have a smaller water area, passageway, and water seal. They are flushed by creating a siphon action in the trapway, assisted by a water jet located at the inlet to the trapway. This siphon pulls the waste from the bowl. The reverse-trap toilet is more sanitary than the washdown model since water covers more of the bowl surface.

- The siphon jet type of toilet is quieter than the washdown or reverse trap and has a larger water surface with most of the interior surface of the bowl covered with water. Generally more expensive than the reverse trap model, the siphon jet has a larger trapway which is less subject to clogging.
- The siphon jet action low-profile, one-piece toilet is the "top of the line" and least noisy of all types of toilets. This model has almost no dry surfaces on the bowl interior. Another feature is the low profile design sought in many bathroom layouts.

The Pull-Chain toilet of Victorian history is making a comeback as a decorator bathroom approach. The floor-mounted bowl is serviced by an elevated tank (sometimes insulated to lessen condensation) complete with pull chain and surface-mounted piping and pipe supports.

The recently introduced rear outlet toilet is especially functional in adding a new lavatory or bathroom in a home with concrete slab floors. This unit permits discharge above the floor directly into a drainage fitting in the wall. No sleeving, channeling or drilling into the slab is required to lay the drain. (A similar bathtub also is available for draining above floor level.)

Regardless of the type of toilet selected for new construction, remodeling, or replacement, the unit must perform a full cycle of functions:
- flush completely and efficiently
- shut off the water flow to the bowl at the end of the flushing action
- refill the tank to the necessary depth and then shut off the water supply line

Tank mechanisms vary from manufacturer to manufacturer, but most units operate with a ball-cock attached to a valve by means of a rod or arm. As the toilet handle is pushed, the water flows from the tank to the toilet as the ballcock drops and the valve opens. As the tank refills, the float ball rises,

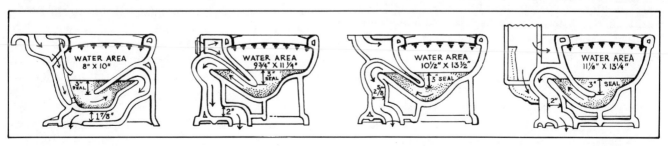

The Washdown   *Reverse Trap*   *Siphon Jet*   *Siphon Low-Profile*

Wall-hung water closets simplify floor and fixture cleaning. This elongated unit is equipped with a ventilator which automatically eliminates toilet odors before they *can become bathroom odors. Photo courtesy of American-Standard*

closing the valve and stopping the flow of incoming water at the proper level indicated by a mark inside the tank. Manufacturers caution that homeowners not set the tank water level below the indicated mark in an effort to save water. A reduced volume of water is likely to provide an incomplete flush and not cleanse the bowl.

Toilet styles vary somewhat from maker to maker, but most have round or elongated bowls. The latter style is sometimes referred to as "extended rim" and is approximately 2 inches longer front-to-back. The elongated is more comfortable, more attractive, and easier to keep clean.

Wall-hung, off-the-floor toilets usually require 2 x 6-inch wall studs instead of the usual 2 x 4-inch studs. These units are supported by heavy steel carriers installed inside the wall and are hidden from view in the finished installation.

Still another variation in toilets is the triangular tank model which conserves floor space when installed in a corner. A 24 x 24-inch corner accommodates most such units.

The Bidet

The bidet was first conceived and used in Europe as a hygienic plumbing fixture which provided a high degree of cleanliness. Today's bidet is merely a low-set bowl that is no more complicated to use than any other fixture found in the bathroom.

The bidet user sits astride the fixture facing the hot and cold water faucets (on the bowl or wall) to wash the pelvic and anal areas. The faucets operate the same as lavatory bowl fittings, controlling both water temperature and pressure. The fresh water enters the bidet either through an upward water spray in the center of the bowl or through a flushing rim which helps to maintain bowl cleanliness.

Typical dimensions of the bidet are 13½ inches wide, 25 inches back-to-front and 14 inches high. Units should be installed in an area 30 inches wide or wider and with a minimum of 18 inches front clearance between fixture and wall.

Most bidets on the market today incorporate a stopper which retains water in the bowl if desired.

Toilet Seats

A toilet seat can help establish the decor for the entire bathroom and thus should be selected for more than its functional purpose. Seats are manufactured in molded wood with baked-on enamel, as well as solid molded plastic. Matching colors are available for most nationally distributed fixtures.

The shape of the toilet seat you select will be determined by the shape of the water closet itself—round or elongated bowl. The lid may be "full size" to "close" the front, or it may be slightly smaller, closing back a bit from the edge of the seat itself.

Aside from the matchng or contrasting color and plain white, today's toilet seat can be obtained with a marbleized finish, sculptured wood cover, golden scroll design, and other decorative designs. Look for coated metal corrosion-resistant hinge posts in selecting a toilet seat. You may also want a seat with an easily removed hinge to simplify toilet and seat cleaning.

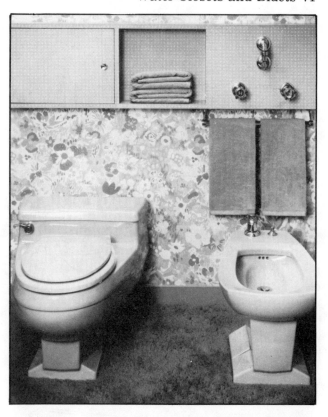

This one-piece vitreous china water closet combination with rounded front bowl and ultra quiet flushing action has been combined in this installation with a 22 x 15-inch bidet. Cabinet contains storage area, control panel for bidet fittings, and small open shelf. Photo courtesy of Eljer

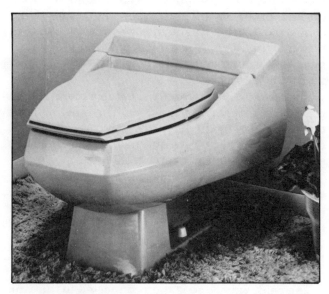

This relatively small one-piece water closet is Kohler's top-of-the-line model and provides virtually silent flushing action. It comes in a wide choice of colors.

Many bidets are made to match the color and styling of most toilets. This bidet is equipped with pop-up drain for filling the bowl with warm water as well as a spray. Water control knobs are located at eye level. Photo courtesy of American-Standard

This toilet with elongated bowl uses a pressurized spray in the flushing action to remove unpleasant odors. The mechanism is contained within the toilet and requires no special valves or pipes. Photo courtesy of Kohler

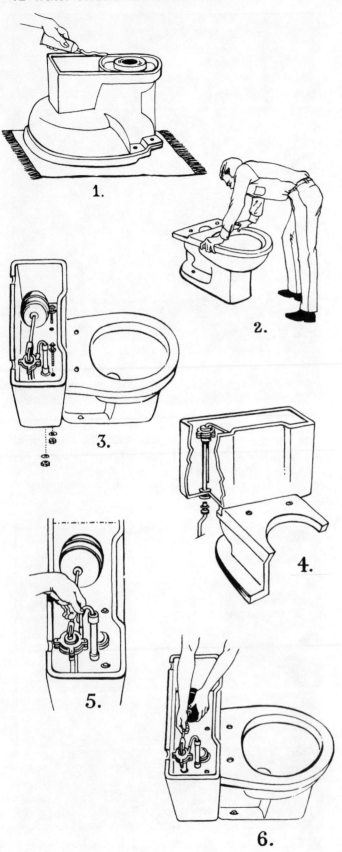

1.

2.

3.

4.

5.

6.

Installing the Toilet Tank and Bowl

Replacement of an existing toilet tank and bowl or installation of this fixture in a new bathroom begins with a thoroughly clean dry floor surface where the bowl is to be located.

The fixture is placed upside down on a protective soft material to prevent scratching (Figure 1) and a warmed wax ring applied to the circular recess in the base of the bowl. This is where the fixture will be connected to the waste line previously plumbed through the floor. A setting compound is then applied to the outer rim of the bowl to assure a proper seal with the floor.

The bowl is then carefully set atop a metal flange previously attached to the floor. The toilet bolts fit through holes in the base of the fixture (Figure 2) ready to receive washers and nuts which should be secured snugly but not force-tightened.

Following placement of large donut-shaped washers on the threaded tank outlet, the tank is placed on the ledge (Figure 3) of the bowl and aligned for placement of bolts downward through the bolt holes of the two parts. Again the bolts should be carefully tightened, alternating from side to side to prevent cracking or breaking the tank or bowl.

The cold water line is then connected to the tank with a straight or angle stop (Figure 4), and the ballcock inserted into the tank and secured in position. This later unit (Figure 5) varies in style with appropriate installation instructions detailed on the package.

Water is turned on by opening the angle or straight stop located beneath the tank. The tank should fill to the "water line" indicated inside the tank. If not, the brass rod supporting the float ball (Figure 6) should be bent until the tank stops filling at the water line. Check the maintenance section of this book for a cut-away view of the ballcock mechanism used in most toilet tank installations.

This toilet is a one-piece unit with a low, unobtrusive tank. The fixture is available with a water system which creates a vacuum in the bowl, drawing air and odors through holes in the flushing rim into the discharge outlet of the toilet, and into the vent pipe. Photo courtesy of American-Standard

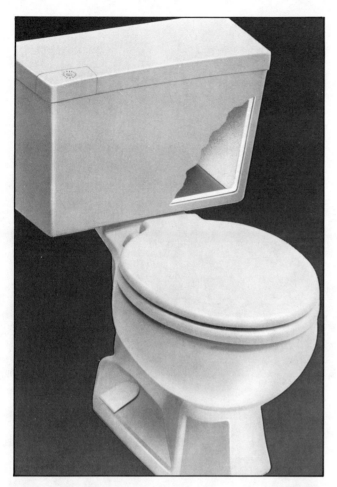

This unit can be flushed with a third less water than conventional siphon-jet units. Photo courtesy of American-Standard

This economical toilet is made of ABS injection-molded plastic and has a corner flush tab which replaces the conventional flush lever. The tank is preassembled and preadjusted, so no on-site work is necessary. The tank contains an inner liner that prevents condensation even under very humid conditions. Photo courtesy of Universal-Rundle Corp.

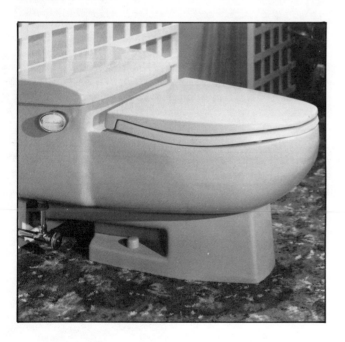

A new vitreous china finish called Earthen Stone is being used in the manufacture of toilets and self-rimming lavatories. The stone finish comes in topaz, jade, and slate. The finish is a smooth ceramic glaze for easy maintenance. Photo courtesy of Borg-Warner Plumbing Products

Saunas, Steam Baths and Hot Tubs

Saunas

More and more American families are making the sauna bath an integral part of their home, and many of these installations are coupled with the master or family bathroom. Discovered by the Finnish over a thousand years ago, the sauna is a convenient way to shed daily tensions and relax tired muscles.

Most modern saunas are prefabricated units which can be quickly assembled in a variety of sizes to accommodate from one to four or more persons. Custom-made units also can be built to the buyer's specifications. Prices generally run from $450 to $1500 or more.

Many Scandinavian families have relied upon the sauna for generations, considering it almost as essential to their well being as food or drink. Finnish athletes to this day insist upon having saunas in their Olympic Games quarters.

The traditional Finnish sauna was a small detached building, heated with a wood-stoked furnace piled high with stones to retain and radiate heat. It often took eight or nine hours to reach the desired 175 to 200 degree F (or hotter) temperature.

A modern sauna can be made ready in 15 minutes or less and provides fully automatic temperature control. In the American version, humidity is held to 8% or less, making the high temperatures comfortable. Some units contain rocks, onto which you pour a few drops of water for a touch of high humidity at the end of the sauna.

Although the Finns use aspen wood, kiln-dried clear all-heart and A-grade redwood is an adequate substitute for the modern-day sauna because of its ability to withstand extreme temperature changes. Redwood acts as an insulator on the walls, ceiling and floor. It diffuses the heat so the surfaces remain warm but not hot to the touch (unless they get wet). Cedar is another popular wood used in sauna construction.

Location of a sauna in a home should be convenient to a shower or swimming pool, as proper sauna bathing requires cold water dousing as the final step. Some families have located the unit in a separate outbuilding, an unused bedroom, a closet, basement or remodeled storage room. Others have added on a sauna bath to their homes adjacent to a bathroom or as part of a cabana adjoining a swimming pool.

Modular and precut sauna rooms first manufactured in Finland over 40 years ago now are available throughout the United States. Units are shipped in sections and can be assembled by one man in a few hours. Both standard and custom sizes are available. Photo courtesy of Amerec Corp.

Standard packaged-type saunas on the market range in size from 3'4" x 3'4" to 8' x 12' and have an inside height of 6'6". Depending upon size, the units come with one to five benches and will accommodate up to 18 persons. Custom designs can be ordered prefabricated for fast assembly at the site. Free-standing floor and wall-mounted electric heaters vary in wattage from 5200 to 15,000, depending upon room size. The UL-listed units are operated by remote controls, or in the case of two smaller models on the market, the heater and controls are built into the door.

Kohler's Habitat environmental enclosure features a cypress deck, four sunlamps, four rain jets, stereo speakers, spot lamps for interior lighting and warm ambience, a heater-blower unit for warm breezes, and a large storage cabinet with heat lamps to warm your towels. A control panel lets you select the elements you want to enjoy—sun, steam (an optional feature), and rain, and the length for each. A thermostatic valve beneath the control panel regulates temperature of water during the rain cycle.

Steam Baths

Steam bathing, or as it is often called, "Turkish bathing," has a long history. Hippocrates, Father of Medicine, reportedly used steam baths in the treatment of fever in 395 B.C. The Greeks considered it a vital part of their rigorous physical education program and the steam bath formed an integral part of the famed Greek gymnasia. This Grecian devotion to steam bathing was adopted from ancient Egyptians who first incorporated bathing into the medical arts.

Today the steam bath is much in vogue although the public Turkish baths which flourished in the 1920s and 1930s have given way to private steam bathing. Units on the market can be installed in a vanity or in the ceiling of a bathroom, or anywhere up to 50 feet away from the tub or shower. No special enclosure is required to create a steam room. Vaporproof and shatterproof sliding glass doors are simply installed to seal the existing bathtub or shower, which becomes the steam cabinet.

Steam bathing and sauna bathing are two separate concepts. The sauna is a high-temperature, low-humidity treatment (usually a maximum of 15 percent humidity). The steam bath, on the other hand, has a high moisture content with its average humidity level of nearly 100 percent. The average steam bath is 10 to 20 minutes followed by a lukewarm or cold shower. Such baths cleanse the skin and invigorate the system. Steam generated for the bath is easily condensed to water by turning on the regular shower.

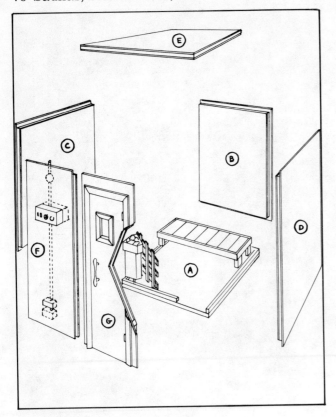

The mini-electronic steam generator is no larger than a breadbox and is controlled by a timer or thermostat set by the bather. Steam is produced within three minutes, and gradually raises the temperature between 70 and 160 degrees, as desired. The only visible equipment is a steam head, which does not interfere with the normal use of the tub or shower.

Prefabricated saunas consist of insulated panels (designated A through F) and a preassembled door (G). The heat control panel is built into panel F for fast connection to an existing power source.

This model comes with precut panels and a variety of optional accessories, such as benches, backrests, heaters, and control panels. The above plan shows dimensions for different size saunas, and materials. Photo courtesy of Vico Products Co.

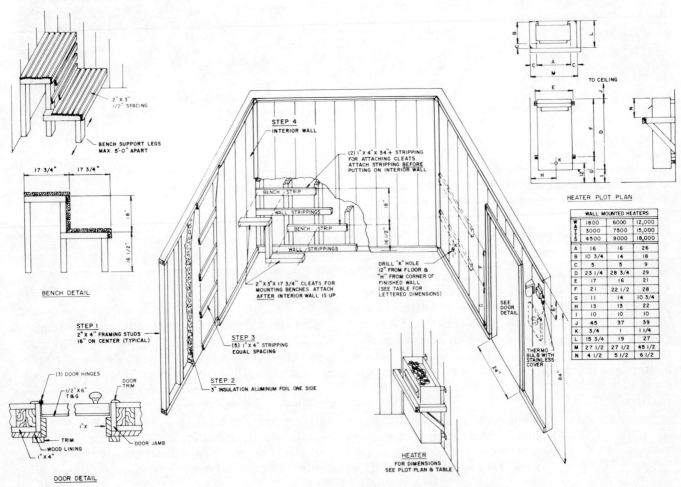

WALL MOUNTED HEATERS		
1800	6000	12,000
3000	7500	15,000
4500	9000	18,000
A	16	16	26
B	10 3/4	14	18
C	5	5	9
D	23 1/4	28 3/4	29
E	17	16	21
F	21	22 1/2	28
G	11	14	10 3/4
H	13	13	22
I	10	10	10
J	45	37	39
K	3/4	1	1 1/4
L	15 3/4	19	27
M	27 1/2	27 1/2	45 1/2
N	4 1/2	5 1/2	6 1/2

Am-Finn saunas are prefabricated and prepackaged in four sizes to occupy 24, 40, 64, and 80 square feet of floor space and to accommodate from three to fifteen persons. The units can be assembled and ready for use in a few hours, requiring no need of block wall or studding. Wall and roof panels are of "sandwich" design with poured-in-place polyurethane insulating core. Clear heart redwood is used for the interior walls, floor, and ceiling. The residential application pictured here occupies a former walk-in clothes closet.

Solo saunas fit practically anywhere. The prefabricated units are 3'4" x 3'4" and stand 6'8" high. Heater, controls, light, and Vent-Window are built into the door. This sauna operates off any standard 120 volt, 20 amp fused circuit. Photo courtesy of Viking Saunas

Hot Tubs

Hot tubs and spas are a California phenomenon that is spreading coast to coast as a growing population finds itself up to its neck in hot water and loving every minute of it. The therapeutic form of relaxation can be enjoyed inside the home or outdoors under the sun or stars. Units may be installed in the basement, bathroom, on the patio or deck, or in an unused area of the yard.

From a technical standpoint, hot tubs and spas (whirlpool baths) differ due to their construction, but both provide the same function—a kind of bone-penetrating, muscle-stretching, nerve-soothing, ambiance in 100-105° bubbling water.

Operationally, spas and hot tubs are virtually identical as they use similar heaters, pumps, filters and hydro-massage jets. Spas typically are made of molded plastic, fiberglass or ceramic tile for freestanding or sunken installation, while hot tubs are constructed of solid wood in tub design for freestanding installation.

The current trend is to install hot tubs in outdoor settings, while fiberglass spas are usually preferred for indoor installations. Both types of units come in a range of sizes with hot tubs taking a natural round shape and spas available in various configurations.

Hot tubbing can be traced to communal bathing in Egypt and Rome as well as the teak ofuros of Japan where families and friends soaked in temperatures up to 115°, sharing conversation, food and drink. In more recent years, these units have come out of the California backwoods to the suburban homesite (as well as commercial establishments) where it is now estimated that upwards of 20,000 units have been installed since 1973 in the San Francisco Bay area alone. Sales nationally are estimated in excess of 30,000 annually.

The concept of a hot tub system is relatively simple requiring a tub of wood or fiberglass capable of handling 500 to 800 or more gallons of water, tube or piping to get the water to the tub, a gas or electric heater to maintain water temperature of 100 to 110°, a pump to circulate the water and a filter to maintain health standards.

Water chemistry is critical in a hot tub system—much more so than in an ordinary swimming pool.

The indoor location of this hot tub was achieved by enclosing a raised wood deck with floor-to-ceiling glass walls. Photo courtesy of California Cooperage

The combination of high temperature and small volume means that the chemical balance must be watched carefully, using a testing kit. One very effective treatment, offered by Purex, involves the use of a granular chlorine concentrate, a PH stabilizer, and a water clarifier. Heavy doses, up to several ounces of each, are used frequently during the first week or so of tub operation. Thereafter, smaller amounts at longer intervals maintain the recommended chlorine and pH levels and keep the water sparkling clear.

The number of hot tub manufacturers is growing at a rapid pace so you should carefully select a company that backs its units with a written guarantee and service. Standards have been established by the American Society of Testing Materials and the National Sanitation Foundation to help insure quality construction practices. There also is an Ameri-

This basement-level hot tub location takes on a "middle of the woods" atmosphere by means of a pictorial mural along one wall. The sliding glass door opens conveniently to the patio area. Cushioned surround above the tub is for relaxing after soaking. Photo courtesy of California Cooperage

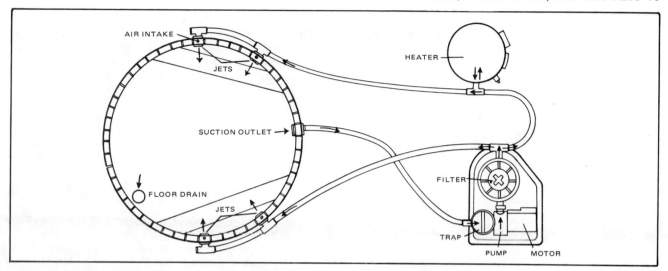

Typical operational elements of a hot tub system include pump, filter, heater, and electric timer. Photo courtesy of   *California Cooperage*

can Hot Tub Association governing marketing practices of member firms.

Redwood, cedar and mahogany all serve equally well for the manufacture of hot tubs as long as the material is selected for vertical grain and carefully seasoned. Most tub makers prefer clear, all-heart, kiln-dried stock (usually redwood) for the staves (sides), floor and seats. The tubs are held together with steel hoops, much like the common wood barrel.

Hot tubs of wood and fiberglass are sold either fully installed or as do-it-yourself package kits. Both methods require electric and gas hookups by a licensed professional to insure conformity with safety requirements and local building codes. A 220-volt service is required for electric models.

Size is the first consideration in selecting a hot tub. A 4' diameter tub will hold up to three persons; a 5' tub up to six; a 6' tub up to ten; and an 8' tub as many as sixteen. Normal height is approximately 4 feet overall with a 42-43" deep interior.

The smallest commercially made hot tub weighs over a ton when filled with water, so careful attention must be given to providing a proper foundation. Wood tubs must be mounted in such a way as to provide full air circulation under and around the tub, with no dirt touching either staves (sides) or the bottom itself. The bottom, which carries the entire weight, rests in turn on the heavy cross pieces provided, called chine joists.

On firm, well-drained soil, several inches of gravel or pier blocks may serve as the base for the chine joists. Otherwise, the simplest solution may be to pour a 3 to 4 inch thick reinforced concrete slab to assure tub stability. A spongy foundation that moves causes heavy torque at seams and joints that can produce leaks.

Some hot tub buyers may still wish to sink their tub in the ground and if they do so, it's recommended that the hole should be three feet greater in diameter than the tub to avoid earth-to-wood contact and also to allow inspection of the outside of the tub should it spring a leak.

Placement of the "support equipment" is another factor in determining hot tub installation location. California Cooperage, one of the largest tub makers, recommends that the pump be no more than two feet above or below the level of the tub bottom and within 15 feet as to the overall length of the hook-up lines. The pump intake must always be below tub water level to prevent its losing prime.

As for protection from the elements, the pump and filter assembly is nominally "waterproof" but will last longer if at least partially sheltered. The electric heater definitely should be sheltered overhead, and in a cold climate must be additionally insulated around the outside to perform efficiently. In fact, in severe winter conditions it should be housed inside, and, of course, your plumbing will have to be protected from freezing. A gas heater, on the other hand, must not be housed or covered over unless equipped with the proper stack or hood and with clearances as specified by the manufacturer. The clock timer and switch usually provided for outdoor use requires connection by an electrician.

Protection from wind, and exposure to sun or shade at appropriate times of the day for your climate, should also be considered in the location of your tub. But since shade usually means overhead foliage, it should be kept in mind that falling leaves and other debris can be a real nuisance. In any case, for the safety of children and to maintain heat, the tub should be covered when not in use.

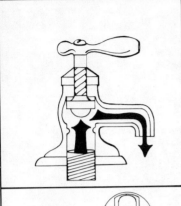

Standard Compression Valve *As illustrated on this page, two-handle faucet sets operate with threaded stems controlled by the handles. The stems screw out to open the supply ports and screw in to seal the supply ports. Known as a compression valve, this type faucet has been around for nearly a hundred years.*

Disc-to-Disc Type *A newer, two-handle type of faucet uses disc-to-disc contact and has no threads. The lower disc is movable, controlled by a standard handle, and the other disc has ports that are exposed as the cover disc is turned. The more you turn the handle, the more the port is opened and the greater the flow of water. Full-off to full-on is accomplished by only a quarter-turn of the handle. This type faucet has no threads, washers, or packing and the o-ring is not exposed to friction or wear.*

Ball-and-Socket Units *Single-handle-control faucets, which have grown greatly in popularity over the past decade, include a ball-and-socket type that operates something like an automobile stick-shift. The lever is moved up and down to control volume and left or right to control temperature. As the lever is moved, the holes in the ball line up with those in the socket.*

Cartridge Type *Another type of single-lever faucet works with a cam that is pulled out to control water flow, and turned right or left for temperature control. The tapered shape of the cam controls the flow of the water by direct sealing of the ports. The interchangeable cartridge has no metal-to-metal friction and is self-adjusting and self-lubricating. If the faucet requires maintenance, the entire cartridge is replaced.*

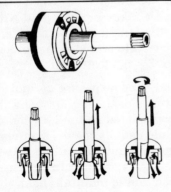

Tapered Cam Mechanism *Another of the newest types on the market is the single-handle unit with a cam that is pulled out to control water flow. The tapered shape controls water volume by opening and sealing ports. Here again, turning the handle left or right controls temperature. This kind of faucet is easy to operate, is permanently lubricated and its single moving part is completely isolated from water to provide years of maintenance-free usage.*

Bathroom Fittings

Bathroom fittings are used more than any other bathroom feature. Faucets, spigots, taps, centersets, combinations and shower heads are all designed to control or direct the flow of water as well as to contribute to the room decor.

Fittings add the finishing touch to every plumbing fixture and should be selected with care. Some lavatory fittings are priced under $25, while others sell for more than $100 per setting. It is advisable to purchase known brands and avoid off-brands and "bargain" fittings because of the difficulty in securing replacement parts in later years.

Most manufacturers produce fittings in three price ranges: low cost, middle price, and a luxury line. Most buyers find the best-for-the-money to be the middle price units, but others who desire the luxury aspect are willing to pay more for the decorative appearance. Lower-priced fittings often can be the most expensive in the long run. The price of fittings depends upon the quality of brass used in their manufacture and the internal operating mechanism. Most fittings now available use all-brass construction in basic parts as this material offers maximum resistance to corrosion and is not affected by strong detergents, alkalinity, or salt air. While most faucets are bright chrome, there are gold faucets, china faucets and faucets made of colorful plastics. Each creates its own atmosphere and may be selected to enhance the total decorative scheme.

There are two basic types of lavatory fittings: centersets and spread fittings. The centersets are one-piece units combining faucet and single-handle or double-handle controls for water supply. These units are designed for installation in single-hole bowls and in units with two holes four inches apart. The spread-type fitting consists of separate handles for hot and cold water supply and a faucet for installation in lavatories with two holes 8 to 12 inches apart. This type of fitting is more expensive than the 4-inch centerset fitting. Each handle and faucet is installed according to the hole arrangement of the lavatory or can be built into the countertop when a recessed bowl is specified.

Shower Controls

The two-valve fitting is the most common shower arrangement with each handle being turned individually to adjust flow of hot or cold water and the blending of both to the desired temperature. The newer single-control valve operates by either knobs or levers which can be moved upward or downward, or in and out, to control volume. The same control is moved to the left or right to control water temperature.

Still newer yet is the pressure-balancing valve which is usually preset to a temperature which is then automatically maintained regardless of the decrease of flow of either the hot or cold water. With this unit, should the pressure of the cold water supply drop sufficiently to cause scalding, the valve automatically shuts off the hot water flow. This type of valve is most commonly used for controlling a shower head.

A fourth classification of fittings is the thermostatic control which incorporates a heat-sensing device to automatically adjust the hot and cold volume to maintain a preselected temperature of mixed water. This valve gives a more precise temperature control than the pressure-balancing valve, and it usually permits the user to control volume as well as temperature.

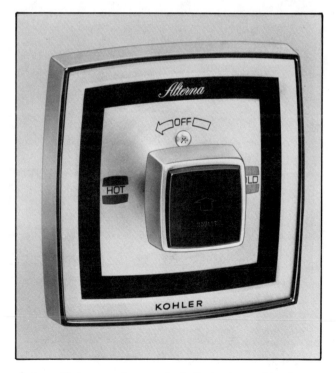

Automatic temperature control eliminates sudden bursts of hot and cold water caused by fluctuations in the available water supply. The unit comes in four finishes. Photo courtesy of Kohler

This shower head provides invigorating needle-to-full flood water distribution throughout flow circle. Photo courtesy of Speakman

Shower Heads

In selecting a shower head, choose a self-cleaning unit that thoroughly flushes the interior of the head with water to prevent possible clogging. If the shower head does become clogged, you can unscrew it and clean it by hand.

Most shower heads now on the market are also equipped with a small knob which can be easily finger-adjusted to select the desired water flow—including needle, rain, flood (for shampooing), and gentle. Some models even provide a water massage by discharging streams of swirling, activated water.

Standard shower heads are equipped with ball joint swivel connections to permit simple direction. More expensive units also feature automatic flow control to limit the amount of water used per minute. This latter type unit is especially desirable in areas of high water costs.

The newest type of shower head offered for both new construction and remodeling is the personal shower accessory which may be used attached to the wall as a conventional shower head as well as hand-held. Equipped with a chrome-plated flexible hose approximately 5 feet in length, this accessory provides controlled body spray, simplifies clean-up, permits localized bathing, is fine for bathing pets, and permits a woman to shower without getting her hair wet.

The inner nozzle on this shower head rotates in an oscillating orbit, discharging streams of swirling, activated water to provide a "massage" during your shower. The cone section slides forward to change the water pattern from wide to bubbly. Photo courtesy of Rain Jet

Harcraft's Crystal Glo shower head fits any standard ½ pipe shower outlet and has fingertip volume control.

Most faucet ensembles come in both spread (illustrated) and centerset styles, in a wide selection of lead crystal, satin gold, lustrous pewter, and satin chrome. Matching styles are available for tub and shower applications. Photo courtesy of Gerber

Push-pull or single-lever operation is optional with these lavatory fittings. The push-pull model (top) has a pentagonal acrylic handle. The single-lever model offers fingertip operation. Both models use a dependable cartridge inside. Photo courtesy of Kohler

Toilet Tank Fitting

Another important accessory for the bathroom is an all-brass fitting which mixes hot and cold water delivered to the toilet tank and bowl. This unit can be installed under the closet tank, under the floor or near the water heater to provide water of near room temperature, thus preventing condensation during humid weather. The unit works in any climate. Some water closets on the market feature an insulated lining inside the tank to prevent condensation.

For ease of servicing or emergency, all plumbing fixtures should be installed with supply line cut-off valves. Should you need to turn off the water to replace a lavatory washer, for example, you merely twist the valve handle under the bowl without turning off the main valve to the house. Access to cut-off valves for bathtub-shower units should also be provided so that they can be turned off. These valves often will be in the wall or in a closet or room adjoining the bathroom. It's a good idea to know where your cut-off valves are and how they work so you can reach them easily and quickly in case of emergency.

Selecting a Faucet for Your Bathroom

A visit to your local building materials dealer or plumber will quickly inform you that not all faucets are the same. Not only do they come in brushed and polished finishes, they also differ in size, shape and basic function.

There are faucets with two handles and there are faucets with a single handle. The more traditional two-handle sets operate by simply turning on one handle for cold water and the other for hot water. To get a mixture, you use both handles and the more you "open" them, the greater the flow of water produced.

Antique lavatory fittings are available in brushed or polished chrome or gold electroplate. Mounting is on 12-inch centers, adjustable to 8-inch centers. Photo courtesy of Kohler

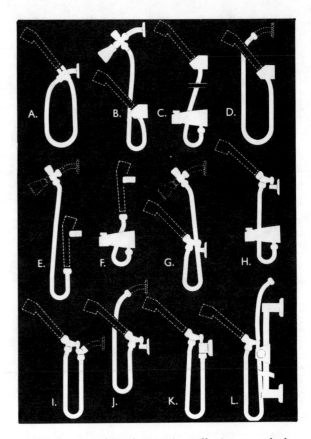

Here are some possible shower installations made by combining shower models, heads, and mounting systems: (A) shower head with an arm-mounted shower; (B) wall-mounted unit for companion use with existing shower; (C) shower added to tub diverter spout; (D) replacement for existing head with personal model; (E) wall-mounted unit added to existing shower head; (F) wall-mounted unit added to tub spout; (G) swivel-type unit added to existing head; (H) swivel unit added to tub spout; (I) swivel-model hand shower added to regular shower arm; (J) shower head replaced with swivel-head unit; (K) personal model attached to supply pipe with elbow mount; (L) hand model attached to chrome-plated brass wall bar. Photo courtesy of Ondine

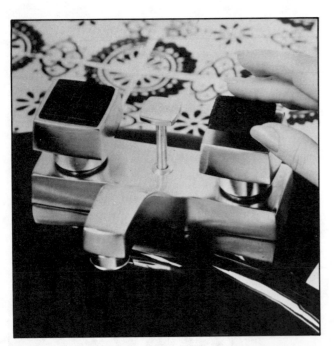

Interchangeable accent color inserts for the handles of lavatory, bathtub, and bidet add to decorating possibilities. Four pairs of inserts come with each fitting and can be changed quickly and easily. Photo courtesy of Kohler

This lavatory faucet provides a soft upward arc of water that falls into the bowl without splashing. The unit doubles as a drinking fountain and aids in shampooing or lingerie rinsing. Fluted acrylic handles control water supply and temperature. The faucet comes in 24-karat gold plate, gleaming chrome, and satin-chrome. Photo courtesy of American-Standard

Medicine Cabinets and Accessories

Just as the accessories added to a new automobile create buyer interest, accessories used in the bathroom as finishing touches often become determining factors in whether a bathroom is appealing and comfortable, or dull and haphazard-looking.

While you have a virtually unlimited choice of bathroom accessories today, you should select items to harmonize with the fixtures, cabinets, color scheme and linens used in the room. Budget, of course, will also be a determining factor.

The basic bathroom accessory "package" includes towel bars, combination soap holder-rail (grab bar) for tub or shower, roll paper holder, tumbler holder, soap holder and robe hook. In addition, you may wish to include a towel ladder or tree, built-in-wall scale, lingerie drying line, combination magazine rack-tissue holder, towel rings, built-in hamper, lavatory-mounted lotion dispenser, safety grab bars, sun and heat lamps, bathtub whirlpool unit, exhaust fan, etc. Basic wall-secured accessories are available in polished brass, brushed brass, chromium, brushed chromium, aluminum, vinyl, antique porcelain, gold-plated brass, and ceramic to match or harmonize with ceramic wall tile. Special heating and warming devices are available to keep the floor snug, prevent mirror fogging, eliminate

water tank condensation, and even warm your bath towel.

Another important contributor to bathroom decor is the medicine cabinet. Contemporary medicine cabinets are a far cry from the sterile-appearing

The mirror of this medicine cabinet is framed in walnut with gold-edged linen inner frame. The mirror size is 14 x 22 inches, while the cabinet takes a rough wall opening of the same dimension. Photo courtesy of Miami Carey

Designed for safe seating in the bath or shower area, this hand-rubbed natural finish teakwood seat folds against the wall when not in use. It measures 18½ x 13½ inches when in use and is anchored with concealed wall mountings. Photo courtesy of Alsons Products Corp.

Real semiprecious stones have been used in the fittings of this bathroom. Rose quartz combines the 24-karat gold plate. The muted pink tone is repeated in pale, delicate rose aurora onyx and marble in the hand-carved bath, with fluted pedestals at each end. The same shell motif was used for the hand-carved wash basin. Photo courtesy of Sherle Wagner

unit of a dozen years ago. Many are tastefully framed in richly carved wood while others have sleek anodized aluminum lines. Built-in units can be as large as you wish and have space for toilet articles, with sliding mirrors to completely conceal their presence. Medicine cabinets matching vanities are available.

Manufactured medicine cabinets can be recessed in the wall or surface-mounted. The units are offered in a wide range of sizes to satisfy practically every decorating need. Most have removable, adjustable shelves and many can merely be turned upside down to reverse the swing of the mirror-door. Still others have mirror doors that tilt for better viewing.

Regardless of the type or number of accessories you select, be sure they are securely attached to prevent accidents and wall damage. Also, be sure to keep radios, portable lamps and other electrical devices or appliances away from the tub and shower areas, where a person touching one could be electrocuted.

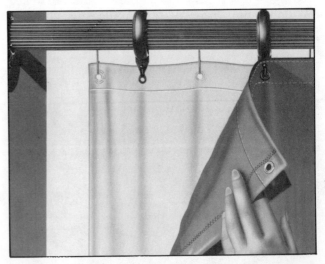

A dual-track shower rod has been introduced to meet the growing trend to use separate lines under handsome fabric shower curtains. Sliding carriers in the back of the rod handle the liner. Separate decorative rings ride in a second track and hold either grommered shower curtains or pinch pleated fabric draperies. Photo courtesy of Kirsch Co.

Bathroom Maintenance and Repair

The old adage, "an ounce of prevention is worth a pound of cure" could well have been written with only the bathroom in mind. For it is here that periodic inspection and a little elbow grease can eliminate the need for future major repairs. Water vapor, leaky faucets and tanks, clogged drains, and loose surfacing materials are the main items to watch for in bathroom maintenance.

Water Vapor

Excess moisture in a bathroom can lead to many costly problems. As explained earlier in this book, vapor-resistant materials should be used and proper ventilation included in all new and remodeled bathrooms. An average shower bath adds between ¼ and ½ pound of water vapor to the moisture content of a home. Tub baths produce less water vapor, but in both instances a little extra effort can prevent harmful damage. The correct procedure to prevent water vapor from spreading throughout the air in the house while bathing is to open the window a few inches at both the top and bottom, or better yet, use a ventilating fan.

Periodic inspection of joints around shower pans, bathtubs and lavatories will indicate when it is time to recaulk the joints to prevent water from seeping into the framing members and causing rot. Easy-to-use caulking can be purchased in self-dispensing containers at hardware stores, lumber dealers and home improvement centers. In homes with crawl-space foundations, check under the floor once or twice a year for possible leaks.

Walls, Floors, Ceilings

Painted surfaces in a bathroom can be maintained with a sponge or cloth and soap, detergent or liquid cleaners. Be sure that the paint on the bathroom walls is washable and always follow the instructions given with the cleaner you purchase.

When it comes time to repaint your bathroom, make sure that the paint you buy will be compatible with the original. Save the label off the new paint can so you can be sure to obtain a compatible paint when it again comes time to repaint. Chemical differences in various types of paint mean that some will not bond together properly. If paint peels off the wall or ceiling, remove all loose areas before applying the new coating.

Walls covered with washable wallpaper or vinyl wall covering are kept clean with a damp sponge. Should your bathroom be decorated with unwashable wallpaper, use standard wallpaper cleaner. Test the cleaner in a corner to make certain it will not remove the color or pattern. If it does, the wall cannot be cleaned beyond dusting with a dry cloth and you may wish to repaper the room with washable material.

Walls surfaced with ceramic, metal or plastic tile can be quickly cleaned with a sponge or soft cloth and soap-free detergent or washing soda. After rinsing with clear water, an old bath towel can be used to dry the surface. If hard water scale is present, a mild acid cleaner may be used for crystalline glazes. If quarry tile is used for the wall or floor surface, it may be kept clean by washing with a neutral detergent. Some quarry tiles, particularly imported varieties, are porous and require a penetrating sealer or finish to protect the surface.

Grout, the material used to fill the joints between the tile, comes in a variety of types including silicone, rubber, polyurethane (only in factory-grouted sheets), epoxy, acid-resistant, ceramic mosaic, mastic, and sand and cement. The newer silicone materials are highly stain-resistant, mildew-proof, waterproof and noncracking. Soiled grout joints between tiles can be cleaned with a small fiber brush and scouring powder or household bleach. More difficult stains may require a grout cleaner. Harsh abrasives should not be used on glazed tile. Ceramic tile should never be waxed.

Cracked ceramic tile is best repaired by replacing the damaged tile. Carefully break the damaged tile with a hammer and stone chisel, clean the mortar surface, spread the back of the new tile with mortar, and set it firmly in place. Permit the tile to dry for a day and then use a wet sponge to thoroughly saturate the tile edges. Grout is then applied in a consistency of thick cream. Use a sponge to wipe off any residue from the tile face while it is still wet.

Cracks or scars in plaster or gypsum wallboard can be repaired with spackling putty available from hardware stores. Patching plaster is used for larger sections of damaged plaster walls, while damaged areas of gypsum wallboard are cut out and replaced with new material. Tape-joint material for this repair can also be purchased at hardware and lumber stores.

Linoleum countertops, floors and backsplashes can be cleaned with soap and water. An occasional buffing with a good paste or liquid wax protects the material and polishes the surface. Use an electric polisher for the floor to heighten the polish and lessen the effort required. To repair linoleum that has become loose, carefully roll the material back to the point where it is securely fastened and remove the old paste from the underside. Check to see that the felt underlayment is securely in place and check also for signs of water leakage, which loosens linoleum. Repaste the linoleum and press it back into position.

Laminated plastic surfaces in the bathroom are easily cleaned with a cloth or sponge and soap and water. Should a sheet of this covering work loose, remove it and, after cleaning the undersurface, apply contact cement to both the underside of the panel and the wall or counter base. Permit both areas to dry and then join them once again, applying pressure with a roller or rubber mallet. Cut a piece of paper slightly larger than the panel to be applied. Place this paper between the panel and surface after the adhesive material has set somewhat. After positioning the panel, slowly remove the paper by pulling from one end. Contact bond adhesive sets rapidly when the two coated sheets meet and thus cannot be repositioned. Scratched surfaces can be repaired with matching-color crayons and a coat of wax.

Plumbing Fixtures

Plumbing fixtures are made for, and will have, a long life when given reasonable care. In remodeling, redecorating or making bathroom repairs, never walk on fixtures with shoes. If you are working or painting around fixtures, cover them with old blankets or padding to prevent chipping. Do not drop bottles, tools, etc., which could chip surfaces.

Hair dyes, spilled cosmetics, leaky faucets and bath mats frequently cause plumbing fixture stains which can usually be removed with a cleanser that will not harm the porcelain enamel or baked enamel surface. Such cleansers are in common supply at supermarkets. Stubborn stains usually can be removed by soaking the area with a weak solution of household bleach or a solution of oxalic acid in water. Manufacturers caution against the use of strong cleansing powders which cause surface wear and lead to stained areas. Harsh abrasives, steel wool and drain-cleaning chemicals also can harm the surface of your fixtures.

Chipped enamel on the edge of a lavatory, bathtub or water closet can be repaired with a liquid porcelain glaze patching compound. More extensive repairs of chipped enamel in bathtubs and lava-

tories can be handled by professional firms usually listed in the telephone yellow pages under "bathtub repair." Cracked water closets cannot be repaired and should be replaced.

Mechanical bowl stoppers on occasion will not close tightly or open as fully as desired. This problem can be eliminated by adjusting the rod "eye" fastened to the pull rod which runs from the stop of the faucet fitting to beneath the lavatory bowl.

Fiberglass plumbing fixtures, while stain and acid resistant, require reasonable care. These units should be wiped with a damp cloth or use soap and water or a mild dishwashing detergent. Never use scouring powders or pads. Minor stains and cigarette burns in fiberglass may be removed by rubbing lightly with scouring powder and 600 grit sandpaper. Repolish the area with automotive wax.

Water Damage and Repairs

Other common bathroom problems can be attributed to water. Most homeowners are familiar with leaky faucets and have at one time or another had experience with a water closet tank that refused to stop running. These problems are usually easily solved.

Lavatory, tub, or shower faucet washers are replaced by first removing the cap nut directly under the handle and using the handle to unscrew the stem from the faucet. At the bottom of the stem you will find a washer held in place with a brass screw. Frequently both screw and washer will need replacing to eliminate the leak. Stem grease, which is tasteless and odorless, can be purchased at plumbing repair shops for less than a dollar and easily applied to stem threads to make the stem open and

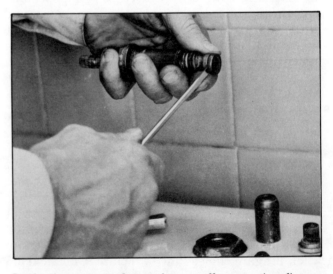

Leaky faucets can be costly as well as causing fixture stains. Replacement of a washer will usually eliminate the problem. Note how the old washer at the end of the stem has been flattened.

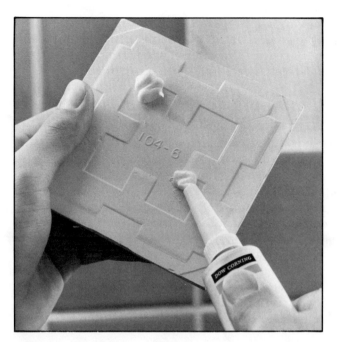

Silicone rubber bathtub caulk can be used to readhere complete ceramic tiles or tile chips as well as to seal tubs, lavatory bowls, and faucets. The material comes in *white and decorator pastels, in handy application tubes. Photo courtesy of Dow Corning*

close more smoothly. Before using the grease, lightly sand the stem to remove any corrosion.

Water seepage around the faucet handle is usually caused by worn-out packing under the cap nut. Use an ice pick or similar tool to remove the old material and replace it with grease-impregnated packing from the hardware store.

Newer single-handle and shower controls use a cartridge mechanism for control of water, temperature, and polarity. This entire cartridge is replaceable in the event of water leakage.

In replacing washers or cartridges, first turn off the water supply before repairing. Be sure to cover wrench teeth with adhesive tape or use material between the wrench and fixture to prevent scratching. Don't force any parts that do not come apart easily.

Clogged drains in bathrooms are most frequently caused by pieces of soap, hair and lint. If your drains become stopped up with annoying frequency, it may be that improper original installation, wrongly sized pipes, corrosion on inside of pipes, or clogged vent pipes, may be causing your difficulty. A plumber should be called.

Lavatory bowls are equipped with traps that can be drained by removing a screw plug at the bottom curve. Frequently doing so will eliminate the blockage or clogged condition. If not, a "plumber's friend" or toilet plunger can be used to clean the stoppage. To use this device, partially fill the bowl with water, place the cup of the plunger over the drain opening and work the handle up and down several times.

This causes alternating compression and suction sufficient to clear many stoppages. A stiff wire forced into the drain opening often works when the plunger fails. Likewise, a chemical drain cleaner may also be used, but the directions should be carefully followed and care should be given to not spilling the solution on surrounding surfaces.

Toilet tank leaks, squeaks, and whistles can be attributed to one or two problems—the water supply does not shut off or the outlet valve does not close. Mechanisms within the water tanks vary according to brand but are designed to produce enough water for thorough flushing of the bowl and then to replace this supply within a minute or so. The accompanying sketch of the most common mechanism found within a water closet tank indicates what should happen when you push the handle to flush the toilet. The rod attached to the handle lifts the tank ball, opens the outlet, and permits water to flow into the toilet bowl. The tank ball then falls back into place, closing the outlet and the tank is refilled from the inlet tube. As the water refills the tank, it raises the float ball which measures the water and closes the supply valve at the proper level.

When water continues to run into the closet bowl after the toilet is flushed, some part of the mechanism in the flush tank is out of order and needs adjustment or replacement. Leaks are usually caused by improper seating of the tank ball. Check to see that the ball wire and rod guide are not bent. Another possible cause of the water failing to shut off when the tank is full is a worn washer in the intake valve. To replace this washer you may have to remove a lever, but shut off the water supply to the tank before doing so. A badly corroded tank mechanism should be replaced.

The "plumber's helper" may be the first step in solving the problem of a clogged toilet. However, instead of the bulb-type suction-cup style unit used for lavatories, you will need a molded-force-ball type which exerts a great deal more pressure.

Leave several inches of water in the toilet bowl and insert the plunger into the opening and start pumping. If the plunger doesn't do the job, you may need a closet auger to break loose the obstruction. If this doesn't work, chances are the toilet will have to be removed from the floor—and it's time to call a plumber.

Selecting Plumbing Tools

The improved design of modern bathroom fittings has greatly reduced the tools required for homeowner bathroom maintenance. Centersets (faucets), for example, are now sold with flexible supply pipes complete with nuts for simple connection to the inlet fittings. this advance alone eliminates the need for a tubing cutter and bender.

Most do-it-yourself plumbing repairs can be made with the following tools:
- Phillips and standard screwdrivers.
- Crescent wrench—adjustable with flat, smooth jaw.
- Pipe wrench—adjustable toothed jaw for use on pipe rather than fittings. Either a 14″ or 18″ wrench with jaws opening 2 to 2½″ is most practical.
- Basin wrench—toothed jaws mounted at right angles to one end of a long steel handle for reaching into close quarters beneath a lavatory to tighten or loosen the nuts holding the fitting in place.
- Adjustable spud wrench—smooth jawed, designed to fit the flanges of unions, valve bonnets, drain nuts on tubs and sinks and other flat horizontal fittings.
- Adjustable pliers—sometimes called water-pump pliers.
- Standard or bulb-type plunger.
- Penetrating oil, pipe joint compound and electrician's tape.

Other plumbing tools such as socket wrenches for removing wall tub and shower faucets get so little homeowner use that it is usually better to rent them when needed. The same holds true of pipe cutters, pipe vises, augers and large pipe wrenches.

Preparing for Winter Absences

When closing your home for a vacation or longer period of time, care should be given to protecting the plumbing fixtures. This is especially necessary in cold climates if the house heating system will not be operating.

Begin by turning off the main water supply valve and opening all interior and exterior faucets and pipe drains. All sink and lavatory traps should also be drained and the toilet bowl emptied. The water heater should be turned off and drained. Some type of antifreeze should then be put into the toilet bowl to keep it from cracking. Kerosene is often used for this purpose.

How to Repair a Toilet

Leaky flush valves attributable to conventional toilet tank mechanism can be quickly eliminated with a Flusher Fixer Kit available from hardware and lumber dealers. The kit replaces the worn-out tank ball or flapper and does away with lift wires and brackets that often become bent. Unlike conventional flush valve assemblies, the Flusher Fixer Kit is installed without tools and without removing the tank from the bowl. The kit's seat is simply bonded directly onto the existing seat with a patented watertight sealant.

As detailed in the accompaning photographs, the old tank stopper ball is first removed from the toilet along with the lift wires and bracket guide (Illustration 1). Steel wool is then used to clean off the old brass flush valve seat and water used to rinse the seat clean (Illustration 2). Waterproof sealant is applied to the underside of the new stainless steel seat ring using the entire contents of the tube supplied with the kit (Illustration 3).

After placement of the new seat on the old brass seat, a 9-ounce can is placed atop the unit to apply necessary bonding weight. The seat is allowed to set in this position for two hours with water level just enough to cover the top rim of the seat (Illustration 4). A chain is then secured to the flush valve and attached to the lift arm. Excess chain may be cut off or fastened to the clip and the toilet is ready for use. (Illustration 5).

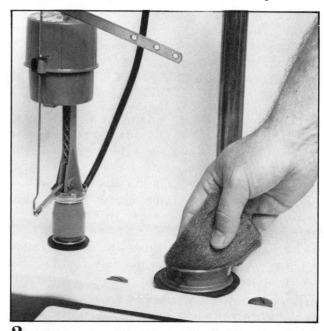

1

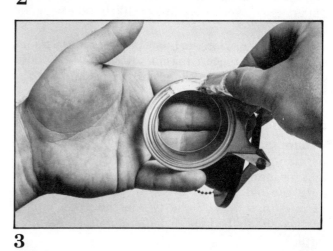

2

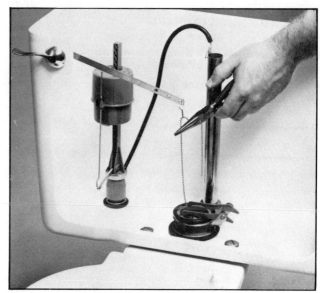

3

4

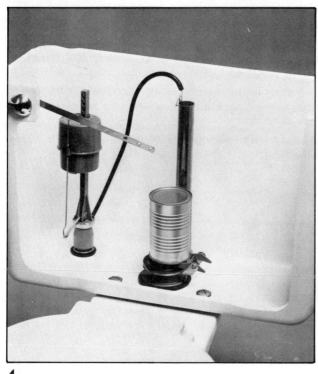

5

Safety in the Bathroom

The bathroom is such a familiar and well used area of the house that we all tend to forget it can also be one of the most dangerous. Here, within a relatively small space, the hazards of water and electricity can combine to cause injury and even death.

Consumer activist Ralph Nader reports that nearly 900 Americans die every year as a result of injuries suffered in bathrooms, and another 187,000 are hurt seriously enough to require hospitalization or emergency room treatment. Falls, burns, cuts, electrocutions—all are possible.

The National Safety Council warns that tile floors are a real threat when wet. Keep them wiped dry and use a non-skid mat on the floor, especially near the tub or shower where there is likely to be water on the floor.

Most fatal falls in the home involve older persons and for this reason special attention should be given to safety for this group when planning the bathroom. But although the elderly suffer the most severe injuries, not a single age group escapes the threat of accident.

Manufacturers are now producing bathtubs with permanent no-slip surfaces, but bathroom fixtures last for many years so that millions of homes have only the old type of tub with slippery porcelain enamel underfoot. Some type of non-skid mat or surface should be provided, along with sturdy grab bars.

Burns can occur in a bathroom. The hazards of gushing hot water to infants and small children are notorious as a cause of death and disfigurement. But even adults can suffer, especially where a too-narrow shower pipe can cause a sudden rush of hot water when cold water is turned on elsewhere in the house. There are simple means to avoid this hazard. The National Safety Council recommends mixer faucets on the washbowl and a mixer valve or faucet in the shower. The most practical immediate step is simply make sure the thermostat on the hot water heater is kept at a safe level.

Electricity in combination with the water sources in a bathroom probably is the greatest hazard of all. Lighting fixtures, electrical outlets, and wall switches all are grouped around washbowls, water closets, tubs, and showers. Persons using this room frequently have damp hands, damp bodies, or are standing on damp floors. Any malfunction in an electrical appliance can be disastrous.

The danger of shock could be completely eliminated by installation of a circuit ground fault interrupter at the fuse box of the house. These are now required in most building codes for outdoor electrical receptacles, and would be a great factor in improving home safety if they were considered equally important inside a house.

Some of the other common bathroom hazards are pinpointed by the National Safety Council:

- Have non-skid mats or textured surfaces in tubs and showers.
- Have a sturdy grab bar for your tub or shower.
- Have medicines clearly labeled and read the label before taking any medicine.
- Keep medicines stored safely out of the reach of small children.
- Dry your hands before using electrical appliances— and *never* operate them when you're in the bathtub.
- Avoid using hair sprays near open flame or when smoking.

Water Conservation

Water shortages incurred in the late 1970s caused plumbing fixture manufacturers as well as the general public to take a fresh look at realistic needs and the necessity of greater conservation of this precious natural resource. California, in particular, suffered a 1976-1977 drought that in effect produced "rationing" and penalties for using more than an allotted quota. The outlook in the 1980s is not much better. Many regions are experiencing severe drought conditions.

Thousands fewer gallons of water can be used in the typical American home with some thoughtful consideration given to the selection of fixtures and fittings, preventive maintenance and wasteful habits.

It's estimated that 425 billion gallons of water a day are used in the United States, this having doubled in the past 25 years. It is further estimated that the flush toilet uses up to 13,000 gallons of purified drinking water to carry only 165 gallons of body wastes to a treatment plant each year.

With toilets accounting for half of all the indoor water used in a home, it makes sense to consider the use of water-saving models being added to manufacturer's lines. Likewise, new water-saving flushing devices including adjustable refill valves, leak-signaling ballcocks and two-way flush assemblies are designed for easy replacement in existing water closets.

Each flush of the toilet, on the average, consigns seven gallons of water to the sewer—so conservationists suggest fewer flushes, especially those used to flush away tissues, gum wrappers, cigarette butts, disposable diapers, etc.

The next step is to cut down on the amount of water used each flush. This can be done by installing a small plastic dam around the flush valve to reduce the amount of water flowing from the flush tank to the bowl without reducing the flow force needed for proper bowl cleansing. Still another method is to insert one or more plastic bottles filled with water (detergent bottles work fine) in the tank. Experiment with different size bottles; if you have to flush twice to get rid of waste, you're displacing too much water. Never use bricks as they can disintegrate and cause plumbing damage.

A toilet can also waste water between uses, as witness the fact that up to 200 gallons of water a day can seep unseen and unheard from the tank and into the bowl. Such leaks can be found by placing food coloring or ink into the tank when it will not be used for several hours. If the color seeps into the bowl, there's a leak and it's time to install a new flush ball or device.

Washing and bathing are next in line in residential water consumption accounting for approximately 37% of the more than 70 gallons used by each person daily, on average, in domestic use alone.

Typically, a 5-minute shower will use 45 gallons of water while a 3-minute shower with a unit equipped with a flow restrictor reduces the amount to 10 gallons. A full tub bath uses 35 gallons; a minimal-level bath 10-plus gallons. Washing hands with the tap running uses two gallons; with a full basin, 1 gallon. Brushing teeth with the tap running takes 5 gallons; with a wet brush and brief rinse, 1 quart. Shaving with the tap running requires 10 gallons; with full basin, 1 gallon.

Shower heads are now available with simple push buttons that turn water off while you are soaping up, then permit you to reinstate the same stream at the same temperature without further touching hot and cold water controls. These restrictors also can reduce the amount of water used during the flow, yet maintain more than adequate pressure for the intended purpose.

Basin faucets also can be equipped with small plastic inserts that reduce the flow of water and aerators (most often found in kitchen sinks, to reduce splashing and make the flow of water seem greater than it is. Some lavatory faucets called spray taps don't aerate the water, but rather deliver it in a broad pattern that is more efficient for rinsing.

A further breakdown on household use of water shows these approximate percentages: kitchen use 6%, drinking 5%, laundry 4%, household cleaning 3%, garden 3%, cleaning car 1%. Combined they far from equal the use of either toilet or washing and bathing water requirements.

Another area worthy of consideration in residential water conservation is water itself. Almost 80% of the United States and Canada has hard water, a fact that costs consumers $6.3 billion annually, according to recent studies by the Water Quality Research Council.

Hard water is said to waste $1.8 billion in soaps, detergents, shampoos and other cleaning materials. It deteriorates plumbing at an estimated $2.7 billion annual rate. It does $1 billion in damage to sheets, towels, linens, and washable clothes. In addition, by depositing insulating scale in water it adds $800 million to the nation's already oversized fuel bills.

Residential water can be reduced to zero hard (less than one grain calcium and magnesium) with an automatic water conditioner. Units can be purchased outright with the owner buying the necessary salt at the supermarket, or water softeners can be leased on a monthly basis for either homeowner "recharging" or regular dealer servicing with replacement tanks.

Water temperature is probably the trickiest energy conservation waste problem in the home. There are three settings on standard hot water heaters: high (180°+), medium (140-160°) and low (120°), with the high setting usually wasting your money. Most every household hot water need can be adequately handled with a medium setting.

Most new automatic dishwashers and laundry units no longer require more than 150° water to operate properly and most personal water usage (showers, bathing) is uncomfortable above 120°.

Manufacturer suggestions for selection of the proper size water heater are based upon the number of bathrooms in the home and the size of the family occupying the home. A 40-gallon model in most instances is sufficient for a family of three living in a house with three baths and either an automatic dishwasher or clothes washer. When the house has both appliances, a 50-gallon hot water heater should be used. The increase to a 60-gallon model comes with a home with two baths, clothes washer and dishwasher and an occupancy factor of six persons.

Water heaters can be easily equipped with timing devices which shut the heater down at night when hot water is not required and then automatically turn the units back on to meet morning showering needs. The U.S. Department of Energy estimates you can save at least $20 a year just by lowering the setting on the heater from 150 to 130°, so the nighttime cut-off would increase this savings.

It's possible to save another $20 a year by insulating the water heater with a wrapping of aluminum-backed fiberglass available from building material outlets. Hot water pipes also should be insulated, especially in crawl space homes where there is often a distance of 60 feet or more of ¾" piping between the hot water tank and the faucet. This length of pipe contains two gallons of water which must be run off before any really hot water comes out. (It's also a good idea to wrap cold water pipes under the home as this reduces the chances of freezing in the winter and helps to prevent warming of the water in the summer.)

Proper maintenance of the hot water heater is still another factor in energy conservation. By opening the plug at the bottom of the tank every few months and letting the water run until it is clear, you drain the sediment at the bottom of the tank that reduces the system's efficiency.

Index

Metric Conversion Tables

Length Conversions

fractional inch	millimeters	fractional inch	millimeters
1/32	.7938	17/32	13.49
1/16	1.588	9/16	14.29
3/32	2.381	19/32	15.08
1/8	3.175	5/8	15.88
5/32	3.969	21/32	16.67
3/16	4.763	11/16	17.46
7/32	5.556	23/32	18.26
1/4	6.350	3/4	19.05
9/32	7.144	25/32	19.84
5/16	7.938	13/16	20.64
11/32	8.731	27/32	21.43
3/8	9.525	7/8	22.23
13/32	10.32	29/32	23.02
7/16	11.11	15/16	23.81
15/32	11.91	31/32	24.61
1/2	12.70	1	25.40

feet	meters	feet	meters
1	.3048	8	2.438
1½	.4572	8½	2.591
2	.6096	9	2.743
2½	.7620	9½	2.896
3	.9144	10	3.048
3½	1.067	10½	3.200
4	1.219	11	3.353
4½	1.372	11½	3.505
5	1.524	12	3.658
5½	1.676	15	4.572
6	1.829	20	6.096
6½	1.981	25	7.620
7	2.133	50	15.24
7½	2.286	100	30.48

inches	centimeters	inches	centimeters
1	2.54	5	12.70
1¼	3.175	5¼	13.34
1½	3.81	5½	13.97
1¾	4.445	5¾	14.61
2	5.08	6	15.24
2¼	5.715	6½	16.51
2½	6.35	7	17.78
2¾	6.985	7½	19.05
3	7.62	8	20.32
3¼	8.255	8½	21.59
3½	8.89	9	22.86
3¾	9.525	9½	24.13
4	10.16	10	25.40
4¼	10.80	10½	26.67
4½	11.43	11	27.94
4¾	12.07	11½	29.21

Common Conversion Factors

	Given the number of	To obtain the number of	Multiply by
Length	inches	centimeters (cm)	2.54
	feet	decimeters (dm)	3.05
	yards	meters (m)	0.91
	miles	kilometers (km)	1.61
	millimeters (mm)	inches	0.039
	centimeters	inches	0.39
	meters	yards	1.09
	kilometers	miles	0.62
Area	square inches	square centimeters (cm²)	6.45
	square feet	square meters (m²)	0.093
	square yards	square meters	0.84
	square miles	square kilometers (km²)	2.59
	acres	hectares (ha)	0.40
	square centimeters	square inches	0.16
	square meters	square yards	1.20
	square kilometers	square miles	0.39
	hectares	acres	2.47
Mass or weight	grains	milligrams (mg)	64.8
	ounces	grams (g)	28.3
	pounds	kilograms (kg)	0.45
	short tons	megagrams (metric tons)	0.91
	milligrams	grains	0.015
	grams	ounces	0.035
	kilograms	pounds	2.21
	megagrams	short tons	1.10
Capacity or volume	fluid ounces	milliliter (ml)	29.8
	pints (fluid)	liters (l)	0.47
	quarts (fluid)	liters	0.95
	gallons (fluid)	liters	3.80
	cubic inches	cubic centimeters (cm³)	16.4
	cubic feet	cubic meters (m³)	0.028
	cubic feet	liters	28.3
	bushels (dry)	liters	35.2
	milliliters	ounces	0.034
	liters	pints	2.11
	liters	quarts	1.06
	liters	gallons	0.26
	liters	cubic feet	0.035
	cubic centimeters	cubic inches	0.061
	cubic meters	cubic feet	35.3
	cubic meters	bushels	28.4
Temperature	degrees Fahrenheit	degrees Celsius	0.556 (after subtracting 32)
	degrees Celsius	degrees Fahrenheit	1.80 (then add 32)